D1600901

Liturgy Reshaped

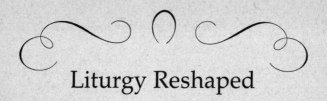

Liturgy Reshaped

edited by
KENNETH STEVENSON

SPCK

First published 1982
SPCK
Holy Trinity Church
Marylebone Road
London NW1 4DU

The authors retain the copyright of their contributions
© Pierre-Marie Gy   John Gunstone   Edward Yarnold
Kenneth Stevenson   Thomas Talley   David Tripp   Richard Buxton
Geoffrey Wainwright   Victor de Waal   Balthasar Fischer
Paul Bradshaw   Colin Buchanan   Donald Gray   1982

British Library Cataloguing in Publication Data

Liturgy reshaped
   1. Public worship 2. Liturgies
   I. Stevenson, Kenneth
   264 BV176

   ISBN 0–281–03865–1

Photoset, printed and bound in Great Britain by
Redwood Burn Limited
Trowbridge, Wiltshire

CONTENTS

Contents

THE CONTRIBUTORS

KENNETH STEVENSON (Anglican) is chaplain to the University of Manchester, and also teaches liturgy in the Theology Faculty. He is the author of several monographs and articles as well as two books: *Family Services*, and the Alcuin Club volume for 1982 on the marriage liturgy, entitled *Nuptial Blessing*. He is to be Visiting Professor of Liturgy at the University of Notre Dame, Indiana, for Spring 1983.

PIERRE-MARIE GY, OP (Roman Catholic) is Director of the Institut Supérieur de Liturgie, Institut Catholique, Paris. He has been directly involved in the post-Vatican II liturgical reforms of the Roman Catholic Church, including the Eucharistic Prayer and the Marriage Rite. He is the author of many studies, a frequent contributor to *La Maison-Dieu*, and a past president of the Societas Liturgica.

JOHN GUNSTONE (Anglican) is secretary to the Greater Manchester County Ecumenical Council and an honorary canon of Manchester Cathedral. He has written several popular books on worship, prayers and charismatic renewal, and a full commentary on the new lectionary of the Alternative Service Book.

EDWARD YARNOLD, SJ (Roman Catholic) has taught for many years at Campion Hall, Oxford, specializing in the history of Christian doctrine. He is the author of several studies on the rites of Christian initiation. He has been a member of the Anglican–Roman Catholic International Commission, and has contributed widely to the development of ecumenical relations between the Roman Catholic Church and other churches.

THOMAS TALLEY (Episcopalian) is Professor of Liturgics at General Theological Seminary, New York. His main interests are the origins of the Eucharistic Prayer and the Liturgical Year, and he is a frequently published author. He is a past president of the Societas Liturgica, on whose Council he sits.

DAVID TRIPP (Methodist) is a minister in London. He is the Secretary of the Henry Bradshaw Society and the author of several studies, including a book on the Methodist Covenant Service. He is also a member of the (British) Roman Catholic–Methodist Committee.

RICHARD BUXTON (Anglican) is assistant secretary in the University of Manchester Careers Service and also teaches liturgy in the Theology Faculty. He is the author of *Eucharist and Institution–Narrative*.

GEOFFREY WAINWRIGHT (Methodist) is Professor of Systematic Theology at Union Theological Seminary, New York. He is widely known for his ecumenical work, and his books include *Eucharist and Eschatology* and *Doxology*.

VICTOR DE WAAL (Anglican) has been the Dean of Canterbury since 1976, following seven years as Chancellor of Lincoln Cathedral. He is the author of *What is the Church?*, and is very involved in ecumenical matters.

BALTHASAR FISCHER (Roman Catholic) was for many years Director of the Liturgical Institute at Trier, and was directly involved in the post-Vatican II liturgical reforms of the Roman Catholic Church. A past president of the Societas Liturgica, he is also the author of many studies, covering such subjects as the patristic use of the Psalter and Christian initiation.

PAUL BRADSHAW (Anglican) is course director in the St Albans diocesan ministerial training scheme, as well as vicar of Flamstead. He is a member of the Liturgical Commission of the Church of England, and examiner in Christian worship for the Advisory Council for the Church's Ministry. His published works include *The Anglican Ordinal* and *Daily Prayer in the Early Church*.

COLIN BUCHANAN (Anglican) is the Principal of St John's College, Nottingham. A member of the Liturgical Commission of the Church of England, he is also well known as the proprietor of Grove Books and for his important contribution to liturgical revision. Among his many studies on liturgy in the Anglican Communion are *Modern Anglican Liturgies* and *Further Anglican Liturgies*.

DONALD GRAY (Anglican) is the rector of Liverpool parish church and a canon diocesan of Liverpool. He is a member of the Liturgical Commission of the Church of England, treasurer of the Societas Liturgica, chairman of the Society for Liturgical Study, and secretary of the Joint Liturgical Group, to whose publications *Worship and the Child* and *Getting the Liturgy Right* he was a contributor.

PREFACE

The essays which follow are intended to stimulate discussion on the many theoretical and practical issues which face the Churches of the West as they begin to take stock of a long and unprecedented era of liturgical change. We have no common axe to grind but this: that liturgy is too important to be taken for granted, and that the hard thinking must continue, so that revision can be succeeded by *renewal*.

In this collection, which we offer to Geoffrey Cuming as a token of gratitude and esteem, many different interests and viewpoints are represented, from historical technicalia to contemporary challenge. My own personal thanks as editor must go to the contributors themselves for allowing me to browbeat them into production, and in particular to David Tripp for the added work of translating the chapter by Balthasar Fischer, and compiling the Bibliography of Geoffrey Cuming's works.

KENNETH STEVENSON
Manchester
All Saints' Day, 1981

FOREWORD
The Liturgist's Task

PIERRE-MARIE GY, OP

A liturgist is first and foremost a teacher, a 'mystagogue', like the bishops who at Jerusalem and elsewhere led those who had been initiated into the Christian mysteries towards a spiritual understanding of those mysteries. Such teaching was first preached, and later became written down, for the benefit of priests in their ministry, monks in their contemplation, and a larger public of ordinary Christians. In the present age, the study of liturgy has become a science which has involved scientific historical method, sometimes brilliantly, most notably in England. But liturgiologists have rarely forgotten that the object of their historical study is of vital importance to the life of the Church. An historian like Gregory Dix, some aspects of whose work may now be questioned, combined the talent of a teacher with the acute perception that liturgy is a tradition which is at one and the same time living and constant; the constant nature of this tradition makes up what he has called its 'Shape'.

The history of Christian liturgies must concern itself both with liturgical forms and the worshipping life of the churches since the Middle Ages, and also with the Fathers of the Church, who are the Fathers both of our worship and our faith. Not every liturgist has to work in these two areas – and indeed, attempting to work in both fields may place the quality of the harvest in jeopardy – but leading Anglican liturgists have managed this double enterprise most fruitfully, among them Dr Geoffrey Cuming.

Since the time when liturgists of my generation discovered in reading Gregory Dix (or even in actually talking with him) what appeared to us the ideal, all-embracing example of our profession, the task of liturgists has been both widened and

1

unified. All Christian liturgies of the present day have discovered in their relationship with ancient tradition the source both of their renewal and of their presence in a world which has changed a great deal. Everywhere, liturgists have become, directly or indirectly, and often without even having tried, the artisans of liturgical reform; not because they wanted to change the liturgy or to depart from tradition, but because deepening that tradition was by its very nature a force of renewal. A nineteenth-century liturgist like Dom Prosper Guéranger, abbot of Solesmes, had been by conviction and temperament a traditionalist, just like his Anglican contemporaries. But the return to tradition which they set in motion was so deep, and in the event so authentic, that with the passage of time it led, by its fidelity, to a liturgical renewal which was so real that to refuse liturgical reform actually seemed like a departure from that tradition.

Everything which could make different liturgical traditions more authentic brought them closer to each other without prejudicing their fidelity; in any case, the best part of ancient tradition belongs to the Undivided Church. One might say not only that liturgical and ecumenical renewal have been closely associated for a generation or so, but also, perhaps, that fundamentally ecumenical convergence has taken place in the liturgy itself. The person and influence of Dr Cuming, as well as this present volume, are sufficient evidence of this fact.

As always, work done gives birth to new questions. I would draw attention to two, of which the first is a question of the history of the liturgy, and the second relates to the task confronting liturgists in the life of the Church today. After Gregory Dix and Bernard Botte, historians of the liturgy do continue to recognize the major importance of the Apostolic Tradition of Hippolytus, but they are now increasingly concerned with what can be glimpsed of the liturgy of the Church *before* Hippolytus, in the great differences that it contained, and in the influence of Jewish prayer. Some of these researches have produced (and can still produce) much fruit in our understanding of the Christian liturgy, but, I think, on two conditions. The first is that, as Thomas Talley shows us in this very volume regarding the Eucharist, it must take account of both the Jewish roots of Christian worship, and (no less important) the specific character of Christian prayer as belonging to the New Covenant. As Thomas Aquinas puts it in the hymn 'Lauda Sion', 'This new Passover's new blessing hath fulfilled the older rite'. The second condition consists in taking into account the sort of synthesis of partly diverse liturgical practices which seems to occur in the second century (at the same time as the fixing of the Canon of Scripture), of which Hippolytus is the first and great witness. In this respect, we cannot go beyond the Apostolic Tradition, even if it is not perhaps as traditional as it claims to be; we can no longer separate the various elements which it has synthesized.

Finally let me return to the duty of liturgists today. They should try to ensure that contemporary liturgy finds an appropriate climate and spirituality; that it is being understood by its ministers and the whole people of God; and that it is seen to arise from the unity of tradition and the way it has been 'reshaped'. Liturgists serve the liturgy, but the liturgy itself is the action of the whole Church at prayer. The work of Dr Geoffrey Cuming, the researches which he has encouraged and inspired, and the disciples and friends which the present volume brings together, show both the depth of his influence and his faithfulness in fulfilling such a duty.

1

The Spirit's Freedom in the Spirit's Framework

JOHN GUNSTONE

Opportunities for local expression in worship are now built into our revised liturgies. Anglican rites, for example, have become remarkably permissive compared with what they have been in the past. The Alternative Service Book of 1980 has more 'mays' than 'shalls' in its rubrics (thus restoring to rubrics their proper function before the canon lawyers got hold of them), and a wide range of choices is offered in the Scripture readings and prayers. The new Book of Common Prayer of the Episcopal Church of the USA has gone even further: it includes a eucharistic rite that consists only of a number of general directions and the words for the central section of the Thanksgiving. The liturgical movement has had similar effects in the worship of other denominations, so that even the Roman mass appears in a great variety of forms.

Such opportunities can be abused, and it is right for liturgists to remind us that true spontaneity can only arise from a discerning appreciation of what worship really is, and of the place of traditional rites and ceremonies in its celebration. Some of us have suffered from well-meaning attempts to create a service out of a newspaper report, a pop record, and extracts from the latest book of contemporary prayers for secular man. Worship needs more than that. It needs to draw on the rich sources of the Christian faith, the Scriptures and the Church's obedient response to the Word of God enshrined in liturgical traditions, as well as on the human situation in which the worshippers find themselves and their experience of God's grace in their lives.

For this reason I believe the charismatic movement is an important and powerful influence in the Church today – in all denominations – since it helps congregations and those who preside over them to do just that. Through the experience of God's grace known as 'baptism in the Spirit', many churchgoers are realizing afresh the meaning of Pentecost in their lives, and this is equipping them, among other things, to enter into creative liturgy with a sensitivity and freedom, a joy and expectancy, that they did not have before.

The charismatic movement has washed up a heap of books on baptism in the Spirit, describing personal experiences of it and analysing it from scriptural, liturgical, cultural and psychological points of view.[1] I do not intend to say more about it here, except to note two results of the experience which are relevant to our subject.

1   The most satisfying theological *rationales* of baptism in the Spirit begin by identifying it with a fuller acceptance by the individual of all that God offers us through Christian initiation. In a mysterious way it is associated with baptism, confirmation and Communion. The result is that most of those who have this experience come to believe that they really are God's sons and daughters in the way the New Testament says they are. 'When we cry, "Abba! Father!" it is the Spirit himself bearing witness with our Spirit that we are children of God,' is a text that shouts with meaning for them.[2] They may have an increasing awareness of sin in their lives, but they also have an increasing awareness of the abounding grace of God. This is relevant to our subject because the voice of the liturgy (all the clearer now that it is expressed in modern terms) assumes that those who participate in worship have this status of sonship. In the new rites the heavy penitential note that characterized certain official texts, particularly those stemming from the Reformed traditions, has been purged and worshippers affirm confidently that 'in you, Father, we are one family in earth and heaven'.[3]

2   Baptism in the Spirit awakens in the believer a greater appreciation of God as the Giver – the Giver of life, the Giver of his only Son, the Giver of the Holy Spirit with *charismata* for the building up of the Church. The Spirit becomes a more dynamic reality in their lives. 'Without being able to estimate all that I owe to other movements of grace in the Church – and my debt is great – ' Cardinal Suenens writes, 'I can say, I think, that I owe to

the (charismatic) renewal a spiritual youth, as it were, a more tangible hope, and the joy of seeing impossible things become possible.'[4] And this is important for our subject, too, because modern liturgical rites have a stronger pneumatology than those they replaced. References to the work and power of the Holy Spirit are made explicitly in such texts as, 'You have sent upon us your holy and life-giving Spirit, and made us a people for your own possession.'[5] The restoration of the *epiclesis* to the Thanksgivings of the new rites has strengthened the sense that, whatever different doctrines of the sacrament there may be, charismatics are drawn together in their faith that what happens happens through the Spirit's anointing, not through the use of certain words and gestures.

Consequently the new rites ring joyous bells in charismatic circles. They are welcomed as God-given aids to enable charismatics to say and to do what they feel it is proper for them to say and to do when they assemble for worship. And this applies, also, to those congregations which have been suspicious of 'fixed prayers'; they have sensed the work of the Holy Spirit behind the labours of our liturgical commissions. I know one flourishing Pentecostal church which uses the eucharistic rites of the ASB regularly for its Communion services.

The bridge between the pentecostal spirituality of the charismatic movement and the formal worship of the established denominations is the charismatic prayer meeting. In fact, it is these meetings which have made the charismatic movement an observable phenomenon in the contemporary ecclesiastical scene. Organized by various groups in cities and towns, they enable charismatics to participate in a style of worship that is vastly different (and often seems much more worth while) than the services in their churches. In them I have discovered manifestations of the Word of God and responses to him in the Spirit that I never experienced in the Church of England. Leading such meetings from time to time (the numbers varying from fifty to several hundreds), I have learned that presidency in an act of worship is as much to do with enabling a congregation to respond in the Spirit with the gifts he bestows on them there and then, as with guiding them through the rite and its accoutrements – which are also his gifts. In other words, charismatic prayer meetings are schools of living liturgy in which worshippers and those who lead worship learn through experience things they would never have realized within their normal Sunday services.

I have listed five features of these prayer meetings which have influenced the way charismatics are sharing in and leading worship in their own churches, especially where the new rites are being used. Although some allowance has to be made for the different ethos in the way denominations worship (though these differences are less striking than they used to be), the lessons are basically the same for all.

The meetings are characterized by an atmosphere of warm and leisurely informality, which is made possible by *a relaxed yet authoritative presidency*. Without a fixed rite to impose its own discipline, the firm direction of the one who presides saves the meeting from disintegrating into confusion as it moves from acts of penitence to bursts of praise, from group intercessions to audiovisual-aided addresses. Usually these assemblies are organized by a team or core-group who meet beforehand to plan the arrangements – the music, the notices, the readings, the counselling, and so on. But everything focuses on the leader. He knows that a certain amount of material is available for the meeting, but he is also aware that the Holy Spirit may move an individual to offer a spontaneous prayer, to say what a passage of Scripture means to him, to begin a chorus, to cry out a prophecy, to ask for prayer for a personal need. Initiatives like these have to be welded into the flow of the meeting. Besides this, he has to be aware of the promptings of the Spirit within himself, urging him to take a risk – like asking the stranger in the third row from the front to give a testimony, or summoning the unknown sick person to receive prayer for healing. Much depends on the establishment of a good rapport between the leader and those present. Then they will accept his authority if he checks the meeting from being led in a wrong direction (if, for example, he doubts the validity of a 'prophecy', or if a request for a chorus is made at an inappropriate moment). Leadership of this kind relies on the spiritual gift of *kybernesis*, 'power to guide (others)', as the apostle taught (1 Cor. 12.28 NEB). The word is derived from a nautical vocabulary and means to steer a ship. I cannot think of a better analogy – especially when presiding over a lively charismatic prayer meeting, when the wind can sometimes be strong!

Under such encouraging yet firm leadership, those who attend gradually gain confidence to participate individually, especially in *shared prayer*. This is another feature of the charismatic prayer meeting. You do not usually have the problem of awkward silences when you invite those present to lead the assembly in prayer! They lay their hopes, joys and fears openly before the Lord and intercede earnestly for all sorts and conditions of men. Spontaneity like this runs the risk of becoming florid, homiletic or didactic, but charismatics learn to be discerning about this. They can blend scriptural or liturgical material with their own words to create something very beautiful for God. On many occasions I have felt that, if their words could have been written down, they could have been printed in books and have competed with the productions of our contemporary prayer-writers.

Two Pentecostal forms of shared prayer experienced in these meetings require a brief explanation, 'a word of prayer' and 'speaking in tongues.'

In a word of prayer, the leader invites the assembly to intercede for a certain person or cause, and everyone begins to pray audibly but quietly in their own way. If an individual is being prayed for personally with the laying on of hands, this word of prayer conveys a sense of corporate support and participation. The muttered words hum like the sound of a powerhouse. Another form is when the whole meeting is divided into little 'buzz groups' of three, four or five, who are then told to pray for one another.

When a charismatic prays in tongues, he offers his voice to the Lord and believes that the Spirit will take the sounds he makes and shape them into a language of praise or intercession. This kind of prayer is generally used in private, but at a meeting an individual will sometimes feel moved to stand and pray aloud in tongues. Then the leader tells the assembly to be silent for a few moments to wait for 'the interpretation'. Often another will then stand with a message of encouragement or a form of prayer – words that are uncannily relevant and enlightening for everyone or for some of those present. The proceedings require careful testing, of course, but they convey an extraordinary sense of sharing together in the power of the Spirit.[6]

Thus those who attend charismatic prayer meetings become involved in the intercessions and praise in a far more personal way than in church services. 'These experiences can reveal a richer notion of active participation than is generally found in the ordered forms of the traditional Churches, both Catholic and Reformed, for whom vocal participation is largely restricted to saying or singing what is prescribed at the moment appointed.'[7]

Because prayers like these are said out loud in front of others, they take on the character of an affirmation of faith in God and help to build up the faith of others. Hence they merge into the third characteristic of the charismatic prayer meeting, *a shared ministry of the Word of God*. It is not only the addresses by gifted speakers that enable people to apply the lessons of the movement to their own lives; other things do this as well. The testimonies of individuals, for instance, reveal how the Holy Spirit leads others through situations and problems in their lives. Verses from the Bible are read out and commented on. Drama, dance, mime, songs and other audio-visual aids play their part. But perhaps most striking of all in these meetings is the exercise of the charism of prophecy.

Prophecies are heard when an individual is moved strongly to announce what he or she believes God is saying to the gathering at that moment. The lives of individuals, groups and communities have been deeply influenced by pronouncements such as these (again, of course, after careful testing). When they are authentic, prophecies bring to the assembly an intense awareness of God's Word as living among them. Prophecies can take something that has been said or read earlier in the meeting and enable the gathering to understand it in a new way or to respond to it with fuller confidence. In these manifestations contemporary Christians are learning both to appreciate the prophetic. utterances of the past and also to look for a recovery of this charism in the contemporary Church.[8]

The fourth characteristic of charismatic prayer meetings is *extended praise*. This is offered through the numerous choruses and songs associated with the movement. Many stem from the negro-spiritual and Evangelical-revival traditions of the USA; others are modern compositions in the 'folk' style. They take their inspiration from biblical texts, with repetitions of phrases and verses, and are set to tuneful and easily-remembered melodies. Tapes and records of them are played at home. As a result, worshippers are able to join in long periods of praise of a free-wheeling kind, moving from one chorus to another, until they are caught up in a form of corporate contemplation. You shut your eyes, fix your attention on the Lord, and join gently in the singing. When one chorus finishes, another begins – perhaps after a few words of Scripture have been quoted by way of introduction. Then a pause... Then another chorus... The effect is similar to that experienced in the chapel of a religious community when its members are singing the psalms antiphonally during an office.

The gift of tongues can be used for what is known as 'singing in the Spirit'. Someone in the meeting begins to sing, using their 'tongue' and allowing the tune to come spontaneously; as others join in, a glorious symphony of sound wells up, voices blending together in rich harmonies, softer and then louder, until the singing dies away as mysteriously as it came, leaving an unforgettable atmosphere of adoration (not unlike what was sometimes experienced at the old service of Benediction).

At some point in the meeting, usually near the end, an invitation is given for those who require prayer for healing or deliverance or help in a personal problem to 'come forward for ministry' (in the tradition of the 'altar-call' of evangelistic gatherings). Individuals come to the front, or raise their hands to indicate where they are sitting, and two or three collect round each, listening and praying over them with the laying on of hands. Soon there are little groups all over the church or the hall; the rest of the assembly remain in their places, quietly singing or praying. Now and then a cry of thanksgiving announces that God has met someone in a new way; one or two fall to their knees, weeping with a sense of joyful release; a difficult case is ushered into a side room for longer counselling. Eventually the leader summons everyone back to their seats and closes the meeting with a final song and prayer. This has been a period of *shared ministry* in which those with special gifts for helping others have had an opportunity of exercising them. It has demonstrated that belief in the 'every-member-ministry' which is a keynote of the movement and, as such, is the fifth feature of charismatic prayer meetings.

What I have described may seem far removed from what happens in most churches. Indeed, a few traditional worshippers, going to a charismatic prayer meeting for the first time, have suffered from what might be called a religio-cultural shock! But in fact the differences are superficial rather than basic. Kevin Ranaghan has pointed out that these meetings are built upon the foundations of all authentic Christian worship:

> It is the Word of God, Jesus the Lord, who invites participants to gather together in his name in response to his invitations. They give praise and glory to God, then his Word speaks further in the reading of Scripture and analogously in the exercise of the spiritual gifts; in prophecy, in testimony, in exhortation, in teaching and preaching. The Word of God works upon the participants in the meeting and leads to resultant acts of even deeper worship, praise and thanksgiving. Thus the dialogue of Christian worship, the invitation of God's words, and the response of his people, led by the Spirit, is complete.

After commenting that the prayer meetings resemble what is known about the celebration of the divine office in the centuries before the arrival of strict formalism, he went on:

> While many of the elements of these prayer meetings are clearly Pentecostal in origin, the meetings themselves stand squarely in the tradition of Catholic liturgical spirituality based on worship as the work of the people.[9]

I have already noted that the charismatic prayer meeting is where both those who worship and those who preside over worship are experiencing lessons in living liturgy which they would never have learned within their normal services. I shall now briefly take each of the five features of these meetings in turn and suggest how they relate to the revised rites and celebrations in our denominations.

1 *A relaxed yet authoritative presidency* When the new cathedral in Coventry was opened in 1962, a shudder went round the Church of England when it was heard that the Sunday morning Eucharist there began with a cheerful 'Good morning' from the one who presided. Now that kind of thing is commonplace –

even in cathedrals. Attempts are being made to create a more welcoming and informal atmosphere for worship. Much depends on the president for this. 'The priest must find a style in which he is relaxed and in which he can feel that the people are being drawn together in worship,' says a recent *vade mecum* for Anglican clergy. 'What seems appropriate to him on one occasion will suddenly seem quite inappropriate in another.'[10] The president's own openness to the Holy Spirit, his authority as a leader of worship, and his inspiration in presenting the liturgical material set for the occasion, must be united to enable the congregation to move through the service, listening and responding to God together. It is not sufficient just to choose the hymns for the choir practice and to drill the servers. He has to be aware that others might be invited to take part – either to give an account of a blessing they received during the previous week, or to be prayed with in preparation for an admission to hospital or to lead a chorus, a reading or an intercession.

These are skills which a *vade mecum* can only suggest, not teach. To some extent it is a lesson gained from experience. As the one who presides gains confidence, he (or she) will begin to feel a freedom in the liturgical role which helps the congregation to enter into that freedom, too. Together president and people learn to follow the Spirit with all the risks and discerning that that entails.

2 *Shared prayer* Even a traditionalist like Percy Dearmer argued there was a place for spontaneous prayer in a liturgy made up of 'the accumulated wisdom and beauty of the Christian Church, the garnered excellence of the saints',[11] and successive revisions of official rites have provided more opportunities for this. Future historians of the Church of England will note how Series Two, Series Three and the ASB were progressively more permissive in this respect. The ASB indicates what parts of the Eucharist may be delegated to others and encourages the president to use 'suitable' (i.e. not set) words. Members of a congregation can be trained to offer their spontaneous thanksgivings and intercessions at appropriate moments during the service so that the flow of the liturgy is not interrupted. A word of prayer can be appropriate during the intercessions; an interpretation following a gift of speaking in

tongues can also be offered at this point, or after the Communion, when the president suspends the liturgical action while the congregation listens to and reflects on the charism. Interventions like these often harmonize with the theme and movement of the service in a striking manner.

3   *A shared Ministry of the Word*   The thematic treatment of the Sunday readings in the new lectionaries has assisted those who plan church services to develop the message each day through hymns, anthems and songs, as well as through the use of mime, dance, drama and other audio-visual aids, together with the sermon. Much of this happens outside charismatic circles (and is not less inspired because of that!) but the movement has re-emphasized the truth that it is the Holy Spirit who makes the Word of God alive to a congregation, not the artistic merit of what is presented in itself. The working out of this truth is more difficult as participation becomes wider. The Fisherfolk realized this in the course of their ministry of helping churches to use the 'folk arts' in their worship:

> It was an exciting time as we unearthed gifts that had been lying dormant and watched new potential emerge before our eyes. In this context our orientation toward competition underwent a transformation. The purpose of the group was not excellence of performance for its own sake, but communicating the Gospel with honesty and vitality. This focus reduced the element of competition in our approach to the folk arts. Though we spent many hours in rehearsal, we were not striving to be recognized as the most accomplished guitarist, or the most talented actress. We were simply concerned that in everything we did, the media enhanced the message.[12]

Like the shared prayer, the shared ministry of the Word unfolds itself through the gentle impulse of the Spirit. The Scripture verse that is read out spontaneously becomes the 'proper'; the testimonies become living illustrations of the theme of the day; the gift of prophecy becomes an authoritative confirmation of that theme, underlining its lesson for that congregation.

I attended a church as a visiting preacher at a sung Eucharist one Sunday. I read the gospel of the day from the pulpit and paused to allow the congregation to settle down before beginning my sermon. At that moment a member of the congregation prophesied. I have forgotten what was said, but I remember it summarized beautifully what I had intended to preach about. For a moment I was nonplussed. I felt as if the Lord had stolen my thunder! Then I realized that the prophecy provided me with an admirable 'text' for my sermon and I was able to refer back to it a number of times as I preached. It was a new lesson in the preacher's role – to draw out *what God is already saying* in the ministry of the Word in the liturgy.

In a large building it may be necessary for the one who feels moved to prophesy to ask for the president's permission to use a microphone. This is a useful discipline, for it compels the individual to check whether or not what he wants to say really is from the Holy Spirit. A number of prophecies were given in St Peter's, Rome, in 1975 during a conference on renewal and in Canterbury Cathedral in 1978 during an Anglican international conference on spiritual renewal. The texts of these prophecies were printed in the official reports of the proceedings.[13]

4 *Extended praise* One problem connected with the introduction of extended praise to ordinary Sunday services is that of time. Most of us have got used to being in and out of church in seventy-five minutes, whereas charismatics seem to be happy spending three hours or so in worship. When congregations learn how to enjoy extended praise and enter fully into it, there is little watch-watching, yet obviously this needs control if the Sunday programme is tight.

Another problem is the aesthetic quality (or lack of it) in many of the choruses which have sprung out of and around the charismatic movement. Choir masters have been known to resign when vicars wanted congregations to sing, 'Spirit of the living God, fall afresh on me'. Yet, as the Fisherfolk wrote, what really matters in creative liturgy is the suitability and authenticity of what is presented as an instrument of worship, not its artistic quality. Joseph Gelineau said:

> The context in which a song is sung ... often has more influence on people's reactions than the song itself. ... The aesthetics of a song is not only to do with the quality of the text

and the music, but with the whole ethos of the celebration of which this song is a part. A very simple tune can be dismissed as worthless if taken in isolation, but can make a marvellous contribution to the spirit and beauty of the celebration.[14]

The fact that a chorus is ephemeral is not necessarily a sign of unworthiness. We live in an age of useful disposables. The looseleaf songbook is likely to be around in the pews for many years to come.

The one who presides has to learn how to steer the congregation through the extended praises, knowing when to let them remain in moments of devotion and when to lead them on to the next item in the rite. In a Eucharist churchgoers are usually familiar with the shape of the service and know when expressions of praise are most fitting. If the singing starts in the *Sanctus*, the president pauses, joins in the singing himself, and then continues the Thanksgiving when the singing dies down. Singing in the Spirit is a beautiful accompaniment to the recitation of the Thanksgiving and the Communion. Students of the history of worship have traced expressions of praise like this to the *jubilatio* of the early Church. Augustine described how a young man named Paulus was completely healed of a disease and stood before the congregation assembled in the basilica at Hippo to announce this at the Easter Eucharist: 'Everyone burst into a prayer of thankfulness to God. The whole church rang with the clamour of rejoicing ... Cries of joy rose up everywhere, "Thanks be to God! Praise be to God!" with everyone shouting on all sides.'[15] It sounds very much like a charismatic prayer meeting!

I showed a Pentecostal preacher the ASB. He flicked over the pages, caught sight of a rubric, smiled and pointed at it. It read, 'From Easter Day to Pentecost "Alleluia! Alleluia!" may be added after both the versicle and the response.' I felt myself blushing; I wanted to explain it, but the only explanation I had seemed ridiculously inadequate!

5 *A shared ministry* Most church services have some sharing in ministry. Others besides the president take part in the liturgy – reading the lessons, directing the singing, leading the intercessions, acting as sidesmen, and so on. At a Eucharist many of the congregation come forward to the altar rail to receive

the sacrament. At baptisms, confirmations and weddings, individuals are ministered to through the use of sacramental signs. Prayer for the sick with anointing and the laying on of hands is common. The ministries which I have noted as characteristic of a charismatic prayer meeting, therefore, are only developments of what already happens.

Like the praises and prayers, these ministries have to be directed to appropriate moments in the liturgy. At a Eucharist, for example, ministries which prepare individuals for the reception of the sacrament (i.e. those which involve confession of sin, deliverance from evil influences, or reaffirmation and renewing of personal faith) should be offered during the penitential or intercessory parts of the service, whereas those which heal, strengthen or commission can be offered appropriately just after the Communion. There is no blueprint for integrating charisms with the liturgy; congregations and their presidents learn from experience how worship is enriched by them. 'Extended eucharists' is a phrase heard in charismatic circles to describe a celebration extended beyond the usual time for such services, but it can also have another meaning – a celebration in which the constituent elements of the rite are stretched beyond the formal boundaries for a wider sharing in the manifold grace of God.

To sum up, the charismatic movement is an important means of popularizing the objectives of liturgical revision – I use the word 'popularizing' in the sense of enabling God's people to discern the Spirit's work in the new rites (as well, of course, as in the old ones) and to respond to his gifts within them so that their worship becomes another manifestation of his presence and power. Then, when the president cries, 'Lift up your hearts', this awareness of God's presence and power stirs the people to reply in exultation, 'We lift them to the Lord'. They know that they are joined spiritually with the ascended Jesus Christ as their mediator with the Father. The pattern of liturgical prayer has become for them an explanation and an expression of their experience of the Spirit. If they had heard Dr Pusey preach, they would have said a fervent 'Amen' to his words, 'Seek the glory of God alone; desire to be indwelt by God, because he is Love and the object of love, and in his love is all.'[16]

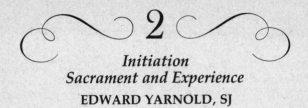

2

Initiation
Sacrament and Experience
EDWARD YARNOLD, SJ

The purpose of this paper is to consider different forms under which the early Church conceived the efficacy of the sacraments of initiation. I am not thinking of the different *effects* which are ascribed to the sacraments: death to sin, new birth, entry into the Church, etc. What I wish to investigate is the *way in which* those effects were understood to be produced. Finally I shall examine some modern baptismal liturgies in the light of these differing understandings.

It seems to me that there were four main lines of understanding; they are however by no means mutually exclusive.

1   Christian initiation unites the candidate with Christ's own baptism at the hands of John. This I call the *typological* interpretation.

2   The gift of the Holy Spirit through the sacraments of initiation is followed by perceptible acts of spiritual power. I call this the *charismatic* view.

3   Through the due celebration of the rites of initiation, effects in the order of grace are produced, which may or may not be open to experience. This could be described as the *sacramental* view.

4   The rites of initiation are performed in such a way as to have the maximum dramatic effect on the mind of the candidate. Because the intention of the Greek and Roman mystery-religions seems to have been similar, I call this the *mystagogic* understanding.

1   *The typological understanding*

This may well be the original insight underlying the Church's adoption of the rite of baptism.

St Luke's account of the early history of the Church suggests that the first Christians attached a crucial significance to Jesus' baptism. In choosing a successor for Judas the apostles looked for someone who 'accompanied us during all the time that the Lord Jesus went in and out among us, *beginning with the baptism of John*' (Acts 1.21–2). Mark begins his Gospel with Jesus' baptism. Luke, while setting an infancy narrative at the head of his Gospel, reserves for his account of Jesus' baptism his precise and elaborate chronological co-ordinates (Luke 3.1–2) and his version of Jesus' genealogy (Luke 3.23–38). Jesus himself seems to have seen a deeper significance in his baptism than that intended by John, perceiving a connection between his baptism and the passion. According to Luke he described his passion as the baptism he had to be baptized with (Luke 12.50); in the first two Gospels he asks James and John if they were able 'to be baptized with the baptism with which I am baptized' (Mark 10.38 and par.).

It is likely that Jesus saw his baptism as the moment when God revealed or appointed him to be the Messiah, and filled him with the Holy Spirit to equip him for his messianic mission. The Father's words, 'Thou art my beloved Son, with thee I am well pleased' (Mark 1.11), echo two OT passages: the coronation psalm in which God addresses his 'anointed' as his son (Ps. 2.2, 7); and one of the servant-songs of Second Isaiah, 'Behold my servant, whom I uphold, my chosen, in whom my soul delights; I have put my Spirit upon him' (Isa, 42.1). With these the early tradition, perhaps following Jesus' own thinking, linked another Isaian passage: 'The Spirit of the Lord God is upon me, because the Lord has anointed me to bring good tidings to the afflicted . . .' (Isa. 61.1; cf. Luke 4.18; Isa. 11.1–3). At the Jordan Jesus is revealed as the promised saviour, anointed (made Messiah) by God as the inheritor of the Davidic promises. In Acts Peter explicitly calls Jesus' baptism an anointing: '. . . after the baptism which John preached: how God anointed Jesus of Nazareth with the Holy Spirit and with power' (Acts 10.37–8). But this of itself does not explain how the Church came to regard baptism as the essential rite of admission for all its members. It is, of course, possible that the sacrament owes its origin to an explicit command from Jesus, such as that recorded in Matthew 28.19. But the more common view among NT scholars today seems to be that, although Jesus may have encouraged his disciples to administer baptism in the tradition of John the Baptist (cf. John 4.1–2; 3.22, 26) he did not found a Christian sacrament of baptism, i.e. which would confer membership of the Church, bestow grace won by Christ's cross and resurrection, and incorporate the Christian into Christ's death and resurrection. It was, it is suggested, the Church itself which, under the guidance of the Holy Spirit, reflected on Jesus' baptism and concluded that a similar rite of initiation should be present in the life of each of his followers. John the Baptist foretold that the one to come after him would 'baptize ... with the Holy Spirit' (Mark 1.8). It was perhaps meditation on these prophetic words, and on the importance of baptism in Jesus' own life, which led the Church to adopt the rite of baptism, understanding it, however, not just in the Baptist's sense as a rite for purification from sin and for entry into a reformed messianic community, but above all as a share in Christ's own baptism.

Early Christian art, in depicting Jesus' baptism, frequently represents it in forms derived from contemporary liturgical practice. Thus Jesus is sometimes represented as a little boy. The Baptist often is depicted as the bishop, standing on the edge of the water, holding a cross or crozier in one hand and laying the other on the candidate's head. Sometimes the personification of the Jordan plays the part of the deacon, standing in the water and holding a towel. 'Jordan' became a generic term for any baptismal font.[1]

The perception of the identity between the Christian's baptism and that of Jesus, which in its turn implied his passion and resurrection, lies behind many NT accounts of the effects of the sacrament. We are 'baptized into Christ' so as to 'put on Christ' (Gal. 3.27). 'By one Spirit we were all baptized into one body' (1 Cor. 12.13). 'We were buried ... with him by baptism into death, so that as Christ was raised from the dead by the glory of the Father, we too might walk in newness of life' (Rom. 6.4; cf. Col. 2.12). The Christian is said to be anointed, a word which, like the anointing of Jesus, is probably a metaphorical description of the gift of the Holy Spirit. 'It is God who confirms us with you into Christ, and has anointed us; he has put his seal upon us and given us his Spirit in our hearts as a guarantee' (2 Cor. 1.21–2, adapted from RSV).

This view of Christian baptism as participation in Christ's own baptism I have called the typological interpretation. The word 'type' has a strong sense here: it is not just a figurative foreshadowing (as Noah's ark is the type of the Church); there is a mystical communion between type and fulfilment. The event in the Church's life is not only in the image of the event in Christ's life, but is united with it and derives its efficacy from it. The fulfilment is to the type as in Platonic theory the individual is to the universal form, both *mimēsis* (imitation) and *methexis* (participation) in the original. A similar belief underlay the pagan mystery religions: the candidate, by taking part in the dramatic representation of events in a god's life, assimilates the spirit of these events into his own life. It is in such a way that Dom Odo Casel's 'mystery-presence' theory understands the sacraments as means of entry into the mystery of Christ.

Cyril of Jerusalem interpreted the sacraments of initiation along these lines. In baptism the candidate's imitation of Christ's passion is 'symbolic' but the salvation received is 'a reality'; 'by letting me participate in the pain without anguish or sweat, he freely bestows salvation on me' (*Myst. Cat.* 2.5). 'So too in the matter of anointing, Christ was anointed with the spiritual oil of gladness, that is, with the Holy Spirit . . .; and you have been anointed with chrism because you have become fellows and sharers of Christ' (ibid. 3.2). 'You were anointed in a manner corresponding with (*antitupon*) Christ's anointing' (ibid. 3.1).

Gabriele Winkler, in an important article entitled 'The Original Meaning of the Prebaptismal Anointing and its Implications' (*Worship* 52 (January 1978), pp. 24–45), suggests that the essential ceremony of baptism was elaborated so as to 'ritualize' the belief that the Christian's baptism was an entry into that of his Lord. The metaphorical messianic anointing of the NT writings was expressed in a literal anointing.

> . . . in the oldest Syriac documents, Christian baptism is shaped after Christ's baptism in the Jordan. As Jesus had

received the anointing through the divine presence in the appearance of a dove, and was invested as the Messiah, so in Christian baptism every candidate is anointed and, in connection with this anointing, the gift of the Spirit is conferred. Therefore the main theme of this prebaptismal anointing is the entry into the eschatological kingship of the Messiah, being in the true sense of the word assimilated to the Messiah–King through this anointing (p. 36).

The West on the other hand, Dr Winkler believes, stressed another aspect of John's baptism, namely purification from sins; the prebaptismal anointing confers strength for the conflict against the devil; it is the anointing after baptism which communicates a share in Christ's messianic anointing (cf. Tertullian, *de Bapt.* 7). In contrast with the Syrian view that the sacrament of baptism is a communion with that of Christ, the West sees it rather, in Tertullian's phrase, as a 'copy of the baptism of John' (*de Bapt.* 20). (Dr Winkler's theory helps to account for many features of early baptismal rites, though it leaves one fact unexplained: why did the Syrian liturgy put anointing before baptism when Christ was anointed with the Holy Spirit after he had come up from the water?)

2   The Charismatic View

Luke's account in Acts of the life of the early Church shows a great interest in the ways in which the Church adapted its proceedings in face of different situations. For example, the long speeches ascribed to Peter, Stephen and Paul seem designed to show how the Gospel was proclaimed in different ways to different kinds of people. (However, to what extent Luke is relying on his recollection of events and on the accounts of eye-witnesses, and to what extent he is giving rein to his historical imagination, is not evident.) The same concern with the ways in which the Church varied its stance according to circumstances appears also in his descriptions of baptisms.

Luke appears to set out his understanding of the basic pattern of Christian initiation in his account of the events of Pentecost. Peter proclaims the Gospel to the multitude; 'cut to the heart', they ask, 'What shall we do?' (Acts 2.37). 'Repent', Peter replies,

21

'and be baptized every one of you in the name of Jesus Christ for the forgiveness of your sins; and you shall receive the gift of the Holy Spirit' (Acts 2.37–8). The order of events therefore is: hearing the word, faith, repentance, baptism, receiving the Spirit. The change from the imperative ('be baptized') to the future indicative ('you will receive the Spirit') shows that Luke means that the reception of the Holy Spirit is not the last in a series of rites, but is the result that can be expected from baptism itself. Unlike Paul and John, who regard the gift of the Spirit as an abiding principle of life in Christ, Luke sees the Spirit as the source of prophetic or charismatic gifts, whose visitation is episodic rather than permanent, and is essentially public.[2]

Luke seems to imply that the gift of the Spirit to the new converts will be analogous to the outpouring of the Spirit on the apostles (compare 2.33 with 2.38–9). But he does not make clear in this chapter the form in which he expects the gift of the Spirit to be manifested. 'Fear' (2.43) may be one manifestation. He may also understand that the routine Christian lives of the new converts are themselves charismatic gifts: they shared their possessions, they attended the temple and broke bread daily, 'with glad and generous hearts praising God and having favour with all the people' (2.46–7). Later chapters show that the Spirit often revealed his presence in more spectacular ways. But, whatever the form, some manifestation of the Spirit is to be expected in every community of the baptized – the Spirit works for the good of the community, not just of the individual. Since the last days have come, the Spirit will be poured out, not only on the apostles but, as Joel prophesied, on every member of the community, 'your sons and your daughters . . . menservants . . . maidservants . . . I will pour out my Spirit; and they shall prophesy' (Acts 2.17, 18).

It seems to me therefore that Luke intends the account of baptism in Acts 2 to be paradigmatic. The accounts of baptism in later chapters either repeat this pattern or show how it was varied to meet extraordinary circumstances.

In Acts 8 the Samaritans hear the good news from Philip, believe and are baptized (8.12). But the Holy Spirit did not fall upon them (8.16). Therefore Peter and Paul came and 'laid their hands on them, and they received the Holy Spirit' (8.17). Later tradition concluded that Philip, being only a deacon, could baptize but not confer the Spirit ('confirm'), as the latter function was reserved to the apostles, who were bishops. This interpretation, however, imposes an anachronistic pattern of organization on the early Church. Luke's point cannot be that there was a regular last rite of initiation for the giving of the Spirit which only apostles could perform; in the following chapter Ananias imparts the Spirit to Paul (9.17). The point is rather that the absence of visible charismatic gifts proves that for some unidentified reason the Holy Spirit did not come down upon the Samaritans as he was expected to come down on the baptized. Peter and John are sent, Luke implies, not as bishops to confirm, but because apostles ought to be involved when the Gospel is accepted outside the Jewish community (Acts 8.14), as this marks a new stage in the apostles' witness (cf. Acts 1.8). The hand-laying which is the means by which the Samaritans receive the Spirit (Acts 8.17–18) is not, therefore, a regular rite for imparting the Spirit, but an emergency rite for correcting an anomalous situation.

At the end of the same chapter there is another description of a baptism, performed by Philip on the eunuch. The first stages are the usual ones: Philip proclaims 'the good news of Jesus'; the eunuch expresses his faith by asking for baptism, and Philip complies. In the *textus receptus* the Spirit is manifested when Philip is caught up and transported to Azotus (8.39–40). But Westcott and Hort's Western text reads: 'The Holy Spirit fell on the eunuch, and the angel of the Lord caught up Philip . . .' Either way, baptism is followed by a charismatic outpouring.

The next description of baptism is that of Paul by Ananias. Paul's vision of the risen Lord replaces the need to hear the word; Ananias lays hands on him so that he may receive his sight and be filled with the Holy Spirit; finally he is baptized (Acts 9.12, 17–18). The recovery of sight is perhaps the first manifestation of the gift of the Spirit; but his preaching is another effect of the Spirit within him, so that the hearers are 'amazed' (9.21), just as they had been at the apostles' pentecostal preaching in tongues (2.7; cf. 10.45). Thus the pattern of Chapter 2 is modified, in that the Spirit is first given and manifested before baptism; the modification is perhaps intended to mark the uniqueness of Paul's conversion.

The pattern is modified again in the account of the conversion of Cornelius in the following chapter. Cornelius and his household hear the Gospel from Peter (10.34ff), the Holy Spirit falls on them, so that they speak in tongues extolling God to the amazement of the witnesses (10.44–6), and only then are they baptized. The change in order has an obvious significance: Peter is justified in taking his revolutionary step of baptizing Gentiles by the fact that they have already received the Spirit (10.47). (The fact that baptism is conferred on both Paul and Cornelius even though they have already received the Spirit refutes the view of those who hold that baptism is simply a preparation for a much more important rite imparting the Spirit.)

The account of the conversion of the gaoler in Philippi emphasizes the convert's faith and makes no explicit mention of the Spirit. Perhaps the 'fear' which he experiences before baptism and his rejoicing after his baptism are manifestations of the gift of the Spirit (16.29, 34). The word used for rejoicing here (vb *agalliasthai*, n. *agalliasis*) in Luke's Gospel is linked explicitly with the Spirit in two of the three places in which it occurs (1.47; 10.21), and is closely, though less explicitly, related to the Spirit in the third place (1.14). The inference seems justified that in Acts too 'rejoicing' is a sign of the working of the Spirit: in the Whit Sunday converts (2.46), and in the eunuch (8.39, though there the word used is *chairōn*).

The events in Ephesus concerning Apollos and the other converts show a new variation in the pattern. Apollos by his fervent and accurate teaching proves that the Spirit has already come on him (18.25; RSV however translates 'fervent in spirit', with a small 's'). Consequently, although 'he knew only the baptism of John', it was not considered necessary to give him Christian baptism. John's baptism together with the gift of the Holy Spirit is the equivalent of Christian baptism.

The Ephesian converts, however, are treated differently. They too had received only John's baptism, but, unlike Apollos, showed no signs of having received the Holy Spirit, and indeed had never even heard of him (19.2–3). Therefore Paul instructed them, baptized them 'in the name of the Lord Jesus', and laid hands on them, whereupon 'the Holy Spirit came upon them; and they spoke with tongues and prophesied' (19.5–6). John's baptism, therefore, without the gift of the Spirit cannot be reckoned as part of Christian initiation. They not only have to go

24

through the whole process, but even receive the supplementary rite of the laying on of hands, which seems to be reserved for cases where something has gone wrong, as with the Samaritans in Chapter 8, who have shown no charismatic signs, and Paul in Chapter 9, who has lost his sight.

For Luke, then, there seem to be two models for Christian baptism: Jesus' baptism with the Spirit in the Jordan, and the outpouring of the Spirit on the Twelve at Pentecost. This is one of the ways in which Luke shows in Acts how the Church relived the pattern of Jesus' life recorded in the Gospel. The newly-baptized are assured of sharing in the experiences of both Jesus and the Twelve: their reception of the Spirit is shown not only in the spectacular gift of tongues, but in quieter charisms, such as rejoicing and teaching; the witnesses react with amazement, as they had at Pentecost.

3 The Sacramental View

The first interpretation sees the gift of the Spirit as a share in Christ's own messianic baptism. The second sees it as a charismatic outpouring which normally follows upon water-baptism. The third view sees it as an interior grace caused by the performance of a specific rite of anointing or hand-laying. In the early third century Tertullian took this view; after baptism 'there follows the imposition of the hand in benediction, inviting or welcoming the Holy Spirit' (*de Bapt*. 8, tr. E. Evans). We have already seen how Cyril of Jerusalem put forward the typological explanation. He also adopted a view of sacramental causality, in such a thoroughgoing way that he seems almost to believe in transubstantiation of the chrism.

> But be sure not to regard the chrism merely as ointment. Just as the bread of the Eucharist after the invocation of the Holy Spirit is no longer ordinary bread, but the body of Christ, so the holy chrism after the invocation is no longer plain and, so to say, common ointment but Christ's grace, which through the presence of the Holy Spirit instils his divinity into us' (*Myst. Cat*. 3.3).

There are also in the NT non-Lucan passages which suggest that, in some parts of the Church at least, there had evolved a separate rite for the giving of the Spirit. For example, the 'three witnesses, the Spirit, the water, and the blood' (1 John 5.8) may refer to three sacramental rites: anointing/hand-laying/sealing, baptism, Eucharist. The 'seal' which is frequently spoken of (e.g. 2 Cor. 1.22) may sometimes be not a metaphor, but an allusion to a rite for the giving of the Spirit.

4   The Mystagogic View

In the Greek and Roman mystery-religions the candidate witnessed a representation of episodes in the life of a god or goddess, and himself took part in the action. For example, in the Eleusinian mysteries in honour of Demeter, the corn-goddess, the candidate seems to have himself re-enacted the goddess's mournful search for her daughter Persephone (Proserpine), whom Pluto (Dis) had carried off into the underworld. Everything contributed to the dramatic effect. The rites, which could last several days, were carried out in an air of great excitement and expectation; the candidate was fasting and sleepless; alternating light and darkness increased the tension. The typological link then between the initiate and the god which the rites were designed to create was not simply an internal spiritual effect. The intention was to allow the drama of the rite to produce an intense and lasting psychological experience of conversion and happiness. As Aristotle understood the mysteries, 'those undergoing initiation are not expected to gain knowledge (*mathein*) but an experience (*pathein*) and a disposition' (Aristotle, frag. 45, 1483a19).

I have argued elsewhere[3] that in the fourth century the Christian rite of initiation, while remaining unchanged in its essentials, was modified in its mode of presentation by the adoption of some of the features of the mystery-religions, especially those features designed to produce a lifelong psychological impression which would change the candidate's life. The instinct which had already led Christians to protect their rites from unbelievers beneath a cloak of secrecy, now gave rise to a formal and elaborate law of secrecy, which later scholars called the *disciplina arcani*. Christian preachers borrowed from the mystery-religions terms to express the 'experience' of initiation, in particular words denoting religious awe, such as *phobos* (fear) and *phrikōdēs* (awe-inspiring; literally, producing a shiver). Ceremonial details were added so as to heighten the dramatic impact; thus Cyril of Jerusalem, perhaps the most creative liturgical reformer of his age, describes the following rite for the renunciation of the devil, performed at night, and presumably in the dark: 'You stood facing the west, heard a voice commanding you to stretch out your hand, and renounced Satan as though to his face' (*Myst. Cat.* 1.2). To increase the impact of the rites still further, in some churches the candidate was kept in ignorance about the details of the ceremonies and was given no explanation of their meaning until the days *following* baptism. Cyril of Jerusalem and Ambrose both set out the reasons for this practice. Cyril explained that 'visual testimony is more trustworthy than mere hearsay' (*Myst. Cat.* 1.1), an explanation which Ambrose elaborated as follows: '. . . the very light of the mysteries shone more effectively on people taken by surprise than if some word of explanation had preceded them' (*de Myst.* 2). In some mystery-religions the climax of the initiation took the form of the contemplation and the handling of a cult-object, such as an ear of wheat in the rites of Demeter; so too in Christian initiation some preachers put great emphasis on the contemplation for the first time of the objects used in Christian worship. This is a favourite idea of Ambrose's:

> You went and washed and came to the altar and began to see what you had not seen before; that is, by means of the Lord's font and the proclamation of the Lord's passion, at that moment your eyes were opened. Before you seemed to be blind at heart but now you began to see the light of the sacraments (*de Sac.* 3.15; cf. 3.11–12; 4.8).

Because the official who conducted the candidates through the elaborate rites of the pagan mysteries was called the *mystagogos*, I have chosen the term 'mystagogic' to describe the understanding of Christian initiation which stresses its psychological effect.

5   Liturgies of Initiation Today

The first five centuries of the Church's history saw the decisive development of Christian doctrine in terms which have been accepted as normative. These centuries were equally fruitful in the creation of classical liturgical forms. Although these may not enjoy the same normative status as the early definitions of doctrine, any modern liturgical revision which ignores them is likely to be cutting itself off from a source of vitality and spiritual power. So to conclude this paper I shall take the four interpretations of the rites of initiation which have been discussed above, and see to what extent they are evident in three modern liturgies: the Initiation Services of the Church of England Alternative Service Book (E), the service for Entry into the Church of the British Methodist Conference (M), and the Roman Catholic Rite for the Initiation of Adults (C).[4]

(a) The Typological View

All three sets of rites naturally contain the belief that through baptism the Christian begins to live in union with Christ – naturally, for such is the obvious interpretation of Romans 6.4. All three rites express this belief in an epiclesis over the water. E: 'Bless this water, that your servants who are washed in it may be made one with Christ in his death and in his resurrection' (n. 16). M: 'We pray that they who are now to be baptized in this water, having professed their faith in Christ, and being born again of the Spirit, may die to sin and be raised to the new life of righteousness in Christ' (n. 10). C: 'We ask you, Father, with your Son send the Holy Spirit upon the water of this font. May all who are buried with Christ in the death of baptism rise also with him to newness of life' (n. 215). All three rites at the epiclesis link the sacrament with Jesus' baptism in the Jordan. It is however only in an alternative epiclesis in C that Jesus' baptism is said explicitly to be the source of the efficacy of the Christian sacrament: 'Praise to you, God the Holy Spirit, for you anointed Christ at his baptism in the waters of the Jordan, so that we might all be baptized in you' (n. 389, first alternative).

Again, only C explicitly links the rite of anointing with Jesus' messianic anointing; '(God) now anoints you with the chrism of salvation. As Christ was anointed Priest, Prophet and King, so may you live always as a member of his body, sharing everlasting life' (n. 224). Ironically this important prayer is to be omitted when – as should normally be the case – confirmation follows immediately after adult baptism. Both E (n. 29, 83) and M

(n. 17), though not referring explicitly to the anointing of Jesus, do at least link confirmation with the royal priesthood.

(b) The Charismatic View

Although there is no reference to the more spectacular gifts of the Spirit, some form of charismatic interpretation appears in all the rites, for they all mention among the effects of confirmation the gift of the Spirit imparting strength to the candidate. C defines this gift as help to be 'more like Christ' (n. 229). The Anglican rite of the renewal of baptismal vows recalls that the baptized are equipped by the Holy Spirit 'with a rich variety of gifts' (n. 101).

However, the need to clarify their attitude to the charismatic movement has led the Churches to make up their mind about such manifestations as the gift of tongues. This has been done most thoroughly, perhaps, by Roman Catholic theologians. They generally reject the extreme pentecostal belief that 'water baptism' is relatively unimportant compared with 'baptism with the Spirit', in which the gift of tongues and other extraordinary charismatic gifts are imparted. They retain the traditional belief that the Holy Spirit is given in the sacraments of baptism and confirmation. But they readily admit that the gift of the Holy Spirit communicated by these sacraments may remain stunted and repressed through human inhibitions; it may therefore be advisable to have some later rite which may help to release the power of the Spirit, which may have been lying dormant since initiation.

(c) The Sacramental View

None of the rites is content with the extreme Protestant view that baptism is only a form of entry into membership of the Church, and confirmation only an occasion for an adult commitment. All regard both baptism and confirmation as sacramental signs through which Christ communicates the grace of his Spirit. As we have seen, all three see the font as the source of new life in Christ. E is most explicit on this point: 'Baptism is the outward sign by which we receive for ourselves what he has done for us' (n. 12). All three rites of confirmation include a prayer for the sevenfold (or sixfold) gift of the Spirit. More than the others M emphasizes that confirmation is the admission into full membership of the Church; but it gives equal prominence in the formula of confirmation to the conferring of the Spirit: 'Lord, confirm your servant N. by your Holy Spirit that he may continue to be yours for ever. (Amen.) We welcome you into the full membership of the Christian Church and the Society in this place' (n. 19). The hymns of Charles Wesley, which M integrates into the rite, at least as an option, also speak of the gift of the Spirit – for example:

> O thou who camest from above
> > The pure celestial fire to impart,
> Kindle a flame of sacred love
> > On the mean altar of my heart! (n. 8).

(d) The Mystagogic View

The aim of producing a psychological impression on the candidate is apparent in all three liturgies – indeed, such is a principal aim of all liturgical revision. All three contain, besides baptism, confirmation and first communion, additional ceremonies to heighten the effect. In E the bishop traces the sign of the cross on the candidate's forehead; there are optional provisions for the giving of a lighted candle after baptism and an anointing after the imposition of hands after confirmation. M includes the giving of the right hand of fellowship; the Bible may formally be given to the candidate after confirmation; there is an optional ceremony of the candle in the rite for children. C contains many more elaborations: the protracted process of the catechumenate, with its ceremonies of transition at each stage; the Ephpheta, or opening of the ears and mouth (optional); the prebaptismal anointing with the oil of catechumens; the white garment; the lighted candle. Moreover, all three rites explicitly allow, or even encourage, the administration of baptism in maturer years, when the candidate will be more sensitive to the symbolic power of the rites, as well as more capable of making a lasting commitment to Christ.

However, none of the rites seems fully committed to the view which Aristotle ascribed to the ancient mysteries, and which the Christians of the fourth century seem to have adopted: 'those undergoing initiation are not expected to gain knowledge but an experience and a disposition.' Western Christians have much to learn from the Orthodox about the way to decerebralize and resymbolize the liturgy, but they need to do it in a Western idiom. Is this a possibility in the television age? Can liturgical symbolism be made to make an impact on the imaginations of people who have become accustomed to the far greater excitement provided by the media, and who take for granted a far higher standard of professional competence than a parish priest can hope to acquire?

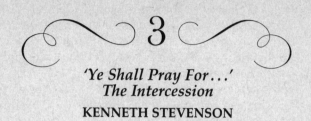

3

'Ye Shall Pray For...'
The Intercession
KENNETH STEVENSON

If you compare the eucharistic intercession in the 1662 Prayer Book with the corresponding provisions in the Alternative Service Book Rite A, you will find it hard to see any similarities, other than the topics for prayer which they have in common. But even this is not entirely true, because the conventional sequence of praying for the Church, the world, the suffering, and (if you are daring) the departed is no longer mandatory in the new orders.

If you look further afield, the new American Episcopal Prayer Book is rich in different forms of intercession, with several patterns and ingredients; and the Roman Missal of Paul VI gives even less direction than either of these modern Anglican compilations. Clearly, to compare the new intercessions with the old is – without exaggeration – like comparing chalk with cheese.

In the face of what amounts to a liturgical revolution, there can be little doubt that much confusion surrounds Christian congregations on prayer in general, and intercession in particular; and it is my purpose to clarify the aims, theological, liturgical and pastoral, which might help redirect contemporary intercession, and, in the process, to discuss some of the problems thrown up by new language in prayer. If Liturgy is the Cinderella of theological studies, then the intercession is certainly the Cinderella of liturgical studies. It is an item of regular worship which is too important to ignore, because it occupies a central position in the Eucharist – indeed, one might almost say that it is the *pivot* on which the Liturgy of the Word moves forward to the Liturgy of the Sacrament: and the current renewal of non-eucharistic worship means that the intercession is no longer, if it ever was, specifically the 'prayer of the *faithful*'.

Furthermore, because of its central position, the intercession has become increasingly isolated. In the old days, it seemed as if the entire liturgy was made up of different prayers, which were jumbled together without much coherence, unless you had a good knowledge of liturgy. Now it stands in stark loneliness, and we often appear not to know what we do with it, largely because we have not thought it out.

The result is that intercessions may seem like A. A. Milne's 'Expotition to the North Pole', in which the Church bumbles along, not quite sure where it is going, and not even unanimous about what it is doing... Put in liturgical terms, this 'Expotition' is a sort of à la carte diet of fancy liturgical experimentation; some enjoy the indulgence, like Pooh-Bear, but others, like Eeyore, clearly do not!

What is intercession?

If much of liturgical renewal is, at its best, a *retour aux sources*, then any theological renewal which accompanies it, however nervously, should constitute a return to *fundamentals*. In public worship, we are dealing with theology, and Regin Prenter was right to affirm once that 'the liturgy of the church is theological. It speaks to God and Man about God and Man'. Reinterpreting the *lex orandi lex credendi* motto attributed to Prosper of Aquitaine, Prenter offers us a stern warning against a liturgy which does not heed theology, and against holding to a theology which is divorced from the praying life of the Church. Nowhere is this tension more acute than at the point in public worship when the Christian assembly offers to God its own needs and the needs of the whole world. *How* a person intercedes is a reflection of what he really believes, whether such prayers are uttered in public on Sunday morning after much preparation, or are the silent, spontaneous thoughts and yearnings of the individual which his circumstances provoke.

Long ago, Augustine wrote that 'God does not ask us to tell him about our needs in order to learn about them, but in order that we may be made capable of receiving his gifts. '[1] It is a sound principle that good theology emerges from Christian life as it is experienced, and Augustine wrote those words to clear one befuddled mind (a woman called Proba) concerning the need for intercessory prayer, which during his time was still an integral part of the eucharistic liturgy.

Intercession is the way the Christian builds up his relationship with God so that he may discern his will, and try to carry it out. This is the exact opposite of the theology of prayer which arises from so many extempore (and prepared) utterances, a feature of Church life which we may with some justification caricature as the 'let us pray – here is the news' syndrome. By all means, 'pray for all men according to their needs', but the danger is that God is presented to the assembly as some power whose mind has already been made up, and it is the purpose of repetitious, intense, fulsome, and even sentimental prayers to *alter* it. But intercession is a means of identification with the world, not an escape, and so there are three dimensions to it which are all vital.

The first is the obvious one – our relationship with God. The Christian spiritual tradition, manifested in the Bible and reinforced in the lives of the saints, is one which affirms that God is our friend and companion. It therefore follows that, just as you don't go straight up to a stranger and ask him for £5, you will not begin your relationship with God by demanding what you want at the time. This is why the classic liturgies of the past do not usually begin with intercession, and, if they do (as in the old processional litany at Rome, or the Byzantine rite), the petitions are general, and do not mention specific ends. Herein lies an important psychological and theological truth – that we understand God better in our worship if we come to intercession after adoration, and in penitence.

As usual, the best liturgies are those which have a structure, an internal logic, which is not there just for tradition's sake. Furthermore, our intercessions commit us again to pray, so that if, for example, we are praying about someone dying of cancer, we are ready to receive God's gifts, and rejoice in a recovery, however temporary, or adjust painfully to the end of a human life. Most intercessory prayers are about very ordinary things, but when we stop to look at them in relation to the real heights and depths of human experience, we begin to see how *ambivalent* intercessory prayer is. We are two-faced, because we are frightened, and regular prayer serves as a constant soothing of that fear into a relationship of love with perfect love. Anthony Bloom puts it this way: 'we believe and we do not believe at the same time, and faith shows its measure by overcoming its own doubts.'[2]

The second level is the relationship with those *with* whom we pray. It is a fine thing that the Anglican tradition insists on a Book of *Common* Prayer, which contains the belief and the prayer of one branch of Christianity. Similarly, the new Daily Office of the Roman Church is called 'The Prayer of the Church'. Again and again, we find the need to reassert the obvious, that prayer is a corporate activity, not just with angels and archangels, but with fellow-Christians now. Human nature has a genius for making prayer individualistic; too many people in the past have spoken of liturgical prayer in the Eucharist as 'Me and My Lord', and clergy still describe saying the offices as 'saying *my* office'. One of the lessons which religious communities have much to teach the rest of the present-day Church is the discipline of being physically near other Christians during daily prayer and worship. Even if monks do not like each other, the necessity of being next to each other several times a day can help them to accept their dislike, and to heal it.

The third level is the relationship with those *for* whom we pray. And it is those *people*, not those *situations*! A peculiar habit of contemporary society is to dehumanize people, until they become situations, whether on-going, crisis-ridden, or processed. When I listen to special intercessions in public worship which reflect these secular tendencies, I often think of the bold phrases of some of the classical formulae, which are by contrast so personal and at the same time so theological. This example is the ninth of the Roman Catholic Good Friday biddings, which is personal in style, yet universal in scope:

> Let us pray
> for those who serve in public office,
> that God may guide their minds and hearts,
> so that all men may live in true peace and freedom.

Effective intercession, therefore, needs to be real to the people who are praying, and also apposite. As Geoffrey Wainwright has succinctly written: 'the test of sincere intercession is the commitment to corresponding action.'[3] You cannot pray for anyone without involving yourself.

But this involvement varies. There are some items of prayer

which can imply activity, for instance visiting the sick. There are other subjects of prayer which can involve no activity other than being better informed and contributing financial help, for instance the homeless of the Third World. The *effect* of the prayer, however, is to make us more Christlike in being open to the needs of others, and this is why those liturgies are most helpful which somehow build into their structures a form of prayer which includes certain widely-spread themes in a regular pattern.

Prayer and Language

At this stage in the discussion, it is worth taking the opportunity to explore the critical question of the language of prayer, since it sometimes comes home with a vengeance in the intercession, because of the freedom that is now generally allowed.

Some years ago, Michael Ramsey made three criticisms of the Anglican Prayer Book tradition. He suggested that it suffered from being too verbose, too preachy and too cerebral.[4] His observations in fact point up three symptoms of contemporary Western man which stand in contrast to previous ages, in particular sixteenth-century England. Taking them one by one, it is clear that we do not like length of speech, because we are naturally suspicious of verbosity, whether from politicians, the pulpit, or from the media in general. You have to earn the right to be listened to at length; you cannot assume it.

This means that modern prayers measure their effectiveness as means of communication by their epigrammatic structure and content, which probably explains why patristic rather than medieval or reformed patterns have served as the models for so many new compositions: and if we don't like the anaphora of Hippolytus, there is still the early version of Basil of Caesarea.[5] But while we struggle to work out a new style of liturgical language which is both incarnate in this world as it is now, and redemptive in lifting us from the quagmire of present human existence to beyond, what we lose in a somewhat arid style we gain in structure. You don't have to be a liturgist to listen to a variety of anaphoras, ordination prayers, or nuptial blessings and hear certain common themes, which are expressed in different ways. Variety is the spice of life, particularly when that life is lived in chunks of common experience rather than superlatives of high-flown excellence that don't speak to us any longer.

Preachiness is the second criticism referred to by Ramsey, and it is probably the most obvious today in all modern services when they are presented and performed badly. What Anglicanism evolved in the sixteenth century appears to us today as preachy, although it did not appear so then. But preachiness we are certainly all indulging in to excess. When a service, still worse a whole liturgical tradition becomes intent on getting at congregations, and telling them what they should believe, or more commonly what they should be doing, worship ceases to uplift, but simply pours out, and that with much emptiness. Many celebrations suffer from piling high more and more 'things' on the congregation's mind, whether in unnecessary 'introductions', superfluous 'welcomes', aggressively activist 'notices', or just ill-prepared sermons and intercessions. As Ulrich Simon wrote somewhat rhapsodically and caustically several years ago, 'God still remains to be found'.[6] Worship must recover some sense of *adoration* if it is to be alive and healthy, and the adoration must start from the heart, and not just consist of words. Part of our problem is that we expect the meaning of things to leap to our eyes and ears, and we no longer like to grow in understanding – everything must be immediate. Furthermore, the anxiety to make a 'totality' out of the liturgy naturally means that many wish to relate the intercessions to the theme of the readings and sermon. There is little evidence of this tendency in antiquity – quite the reverse, in fact – and Paul De Clerck's magisterial study of the intercession in the West singles out this modern trend as being a quite new feature of liturgy.[7] Many are the occasions when it is both appropriate and praiseworthy, but there is a danger of making the intercession into a repeat performance of the sermon, with the result that the liturgy loses some much-needed subtlety, the *universal* dimension of prayer is lost, and it ceases to be prayerful. Worship needs more care, more preparation; not least in the intercession. To borrow Bernard's well-known image, it needs to become more like a bowl, and less like a funnel.

This naturally brings us to Ramsey's third criticism, the cerebral aspect of worship. Once again, it is a mistake which can be as easily identified today as in sixteenth-century England. Are modern liturgies, or, more accurately, are the ways modern liturgies are *presented*, too cerebral, too much addressed to the *mind* of the people, and insufficiently addressed to the *heart*? There is a danger of liturgical language becoming too literalistic in its style, and failing to give birth to new images. The Prayer Book Eucharist and the Tridentine Mass in time developed extraneous compensations, but these proved inadequate (as in the case of sentimental Anglican hymnody), or else downright distorting (as in the case of individual Roman devotions). This state of things becomes intolerable because of its theological inconsistency.

Christian worship at its best leans on the wholesome psychology of Judaism: 'Thou shalt love the Lord thy God with all thy *heart*, and with all thy *soul*, and with all thy *mind*, and with all thy *strength*.' The sophisticated Westerner can find this hard to take, but William Temple was right in pointing out that, when religion neglects one part of the human personality, that aspect is bound to return in a disfigured, even a warped form.[8] This means that liturgical language, as well as the style of the liturgical celebration, should evoke a response from the imagination and the affections, as well as the will and the intellect. As long as they fail to do this, our rites and our services will continue to be noted for dull competence rather than sparkling brilliance. The acid test is really that language in worship should identify with the worshippers but also 'stretch' them; it should speak to the people but also uplift them.

What are implications of this for liturgical intercession? Simply this: intercessions are frequently the most verbose, the most preachy and the most cerebral ingredients in the eucharistic celebration, and this holds good also of non-eucharistic worship. This is because they are longwinded, in that they hammer home ideas instead of suggesting them; because they are written (or uttered) in order to needle people, instead of trying to help them to pray; and because they are baldly intellectual, in that they hand out information and nothing more. Of course there are occasions when one or other of these aspects is needed, particularly if local circumstances make it appropriate, e.g. willingness to spend money on an extra organ-stop after a sparse Christian Aid Week. But these heavy possibilites of intercession should not become the norm. Benedict was right in recommending that prayers are better when they are short. Dean Perry was justified in criticizing the old Absolution in Morning and Evening Prayer for containing 'hardly anything except information'. And the Psalmist cried in despair not for a new mind but for a new heart . . .[9]

The liturgy, however, has to carry a great deal. While theologians may challenge any number of traditional dogmas or details of biblical exegesis, *and* get away with it, the moment a change is made in public worship, questions are asked. A theologian's blunder has far fewer repercussions than a liturgist's; and, what is more, liturgy is where most people receive and digest their theology, for good or ill. The hand-shake or bear-hug (enjoyed or disliked) at the Peace expresses forgiveness and reconciliation as the prelude to the Eucharist; and a sweet hymn to the cross encapsulates personal feeling about the atonement more effectively than a series of challenging sermons. Prayer from the heart is the mirror of what we really believe; as De Boer has bluntly put it, 'the most adequate prayer will be the silent prayer, for when we are silent we are one, and when we speak we are two'.[10]

This line of thinking has its advantages, but it also has its drawbacks. It is possible – and probably frequent – that people use the language of the Church to hide behind, and in the old days, the hieratic language of Tudor England or medieval Rome served as a kind of cushion from the self-exploration (even the self-examination) which the plainness of new language inevitably provokes. For example, Anglicans could have difficulties over passages from the Nicene Creed (which, after all, was written in the fourth century, and takes no account of theological development in the many centuries since), but these were concealed, deliberately or not, beneath the subtle combination of Cranmerian prose and Merbecke's chant.[11] The so-called new translation when it is *said* has a different feel altogether, and makes the most somnolescent believer wake up!

But the tension may go deeper still, and consist of a dichotomy between faith as it has been handed down, and belief as it is actually experienced. Anglicans have long been used to this schizophrenia,[12] which often appears in church-members as well as theologians and clergy, whose personal *belief* is radical and questioning, but whose *spirituality* is formal and conservative. It may well be only in the public intercession of the Church that these two contrary aspects can resolve themselves. The great high-flown periods of the anaphora can pass over their heads and hearts, but new-style intercessions, which often insist on particularity, cannot escape their critical eye. Intercession is for them, for everyone, near the bone – and rightly so.

Another way in which people can hide from their doubts through using old language is coming to light in the protest against what many call the 'absence of mystery' in new services. It is difficult to define what is meant by this phrase. It may be lack of dignity, even lack of the security which time-honoured forms possess. The Canon was muttered after the ringing of the Sanctus bell at a far altar; or the Prayer for the Church Militant was enunciated by an urbane and cultured gentleman who happened to be ordained. Yes – we have lost something; but I suspect that much of this 'mystery' (so called) is really about atmosphere in worship – where people sit, how the church is lit, the pace at which prayers are read or chanted, as well as the tone of voice used by those conducting the service. All this, and much more, has changed in so many churches alongside the change in liturgical language. Many people do yearn for the old days, and they probably would have done the same in 1549 had they been alive then. They certainly have their predecessors.

But the pilgrim Church has to go forward on its way, and pitch its tent in new and often quite unfamiliar territory. The circumstances which we mention in our intercessions are different from the past. We are experiencing the hand of God in our worship in consequently different ways from, say, fourth-century Syria, eighth-century France, sixteenth-century Germany, just to take three formative eras in the history of the Church. We may have lost out on beauty of language, but this is a subjective matter in many ways, and in any case, beauty is a deceptive companion in the quest for truth, and many criticisms of new services could be met by preparing and presenting them with greater care.

Liturgical Styles and Tendencies

Paul De Clerck's study of the development of the intercession in the West has thrown a great deal of light on the forces which helped to shape this too long neglected ingredient in the Eucharist. It is, perhaps, a pity that the energies of liturgists should have been so much focused recently on the eucharistic prayer, for although the fruits of their labours speak for themselves in the consensus which is now so apparent between the churches on what should make up an anaphora, more study of intercession in the past before the recent revisions might have helped to clarify aims and scrutinize texts.

None the less, many of the intercessions in the new books have drawn on ancient models, Latin as well as Byzantine (as witness the new American Prayer Book), but never to the point of anachronism.[13] You can pray an antiquarian anaphora more easily than an intercession, especially if the former employs a rich biblical catalogue of creation and redemption motifs, and the latter prays for non-existent catechumens and the Holy Roman Emperor.

Four tendencies can be discerned in modern intercessions. They overlap, but they are still distinct.

The first is the tendency to *particularize*, to which we have already alluded. A glance at contemporary texts proves this immediately, as witness the occurrence of the word 'particular'. We are more likely to pray for the postman's sore toe than for the ailments of Her Majesty's public servants. Like the diptychs of old, particular intercessions have a specific reference, but the danger is that they fossilize, they lose their particularity, because they are unthinkingly repeated.

Particular intercessions of this kind come in two quite different forms, and should not be confused. Pray for Zimbabwe by praying to God, or by asking the congregation; in other words, it is a case of using either the petition ('we pray for . . .'), or the bidding ('Let us pray for . . .'). The biddings/collects sequence from the Roman Good Friday service makes this plain and clear.

Another tendency is to *generalize*. Although not so fashionable, it is still a framework behind prayers of intercession which allow for both 'free' and 'set' portions, and this is the method which was espoused in the Church of England Series 2 and 3 Eucharists. Whether or not these options are always used, they serve to universalize the scope of the intercessions, and may also prevent the community from becoming too bound up in its own pet concerns. Generalizing intercessions are in the same *genre* as the ancient collect.

It is a pity, however, if the free compositions of modern intercessions are invariably particular, never general. The new Roman 'Divine Office' contains many fine litanies at Morning and Evening Prayer which are frequently general in style, meditating on the theological mystery of the day or occasion, a most successful feature, which often combines succinctness with force. At Christmas and Easter, there are opportunities in the Eucharist to bring theology into intercessions, for example in commemorating the dead on Easter Day.

A third feature is to *combine word and prayer*. Not so common as the others, this method requires skill and flair, qualities not in abundance. If the occasion demands, the leader of the intercession may wish to direct attention to a specific theme or problem by a short 'sentence' (whether taken from Scripture or a Christian writer, or composed for the occasion); and it is followed by a silence, and a short collect-type prayer. (The procedure can be repeated, over a number of topics, or different aspects of the same theme.) Such a scheme has much in common with the old Embertide biddings between the readings, or the Hispanic 'Paschal Prayers'. The similarity is that readings provoke prayer; the difference is that these readings should be short and to the point.

The fourth tendency is by far the most distinctive in recent centuries, *involvement*; it is indeed a mark of the revolution which has happened so quickly. The intercession is split up among different participants, who exercise a diaconal function, and the prayers are summed up in a series of prayers or a final collect by the president. Taking this a stage further, the intercession may contain a number of responses said or sung by the congregation, like the *Kyrie eleison* of old; or the responses may be different each time, and easily followed because printing service-sheets is much easier than it was.

History has its own lessons to teach about this. The responses should be real responses to prayer, and not become an excuse to sing elaborate chants, unless the talent is obvious and appropriate. Different voices should blend together, so that the congregation does not get so distracted that the intercession is no prayer, but like a bad chorus from a Greek tragedy. The principle of involvement is a fine one, and needs to be worked at.

Of these four types, the first is probably going to be the commonest for the foreseeable future, together with the fourth, precisely because of the scope that it gives. But they need to be kept in balance, so that general universalizes particular, and monologue tempers involvement. It is interesting to note that Geoffrey Willis, in his study of the Good Friday prayers, has demonstrated that the biddings are older than the collects, and probably date back as far as the third century.[14] Here is a remarkable testimony to the reluctance of intercession to adapt to new ways on special occasions. But where the litany adapted on ordinary occasions, the local rites of Western Europe were very much in the hands of local liturgists, and De Clerck's work on the Franco-Gallican *dicamus omnes* shows how risky is the business of linking set intercessions closely to a particular age, especially if subsequent ages are less interested in development and change, and slavishly use forms which no longer have meaning for them.

Yet another area of development today is clearly a minority interest, but sound and pastoral, and this is to *introduce intercession into the anaphora*. Daring are the churches which do this, particularly if they allow liberty as well. The new Roman anaphoras contain intercessions, but in relatively set forms, whereas the 'Common Eucharistic Prayer' (Prayer D in the American Prayer Book) is the most significant contemporary example, in which there is a structure with (mandatory) general themes, to which may be added special subjects *ad libitum*. Engberding made the study of Eastern anaphoras his life's work, and has shown that it is precisely in the intercession that the various local versions of the prayer of St Basil (on which Prayer D is based) exhibit the most variety, because a number of local styles and interests were in operation in this part of the anaphora as it was reaching a developed form, whether in Syria, Byzantium, Alexandria or Armenia.[15] This should encourage rather than inhibit us, whether in the direction of appropriate freedom, or in order to recover the practice of anaphoral intercession, which is so logical after the communion epiclesis, when the Church prays for the blessing of the Spirit on its life of faith.

Whatever form is used for intercession (litany, biddings and/

or collects, free prayer), history demonstrates the advantages of having a big pastoral heart, in praying for real needs (e.g. the Stowe Missal, which is the first extant litany composed in Latin), and combining this with a good selection of topics (e.g. the *Deprecatio Gelasii*, one of the finest forms of intercession in antiquity). Another lesson is that – as with so many parts of the liturgy – good forms of intercession spread from one place to another on their own inherent quality, and (given imaginative handling) adapt to local circumstances. The history of Christian worship is a nervous compendium of progress and regression, and even if the intercession has to embody on its way theologies which become outdated (e.g. praying selfishly for good weather, knowing that scientifically this makes things difficult for other inhabitants of the earth!), the fact remains that at its best it continues to set before God's people their work and his work, in ways that are sound and clear.

Some Pastoral Issues

Apart from problems which arise from liturgical technique, there are some basic personal conditions which the public prayer of the Church has to carry, and these become more acute with the introduction of freer forms of intercession.

One is the old question of *unanswered prayer*. Intercessions which repeatedly mention people by name, and their physical, mental or spiritual condition, run the risk of demanding from God what he may not give. For instance, if we pray for a regular communicant of the church who is seriously ill, the feelings aroused in the eucharistic gathering may be high, even emotional, and everyone naturally wants him to recover. A diagnosis of 'terminal illness' may lead to the ministry of the laying-on of hands, and anointing (if these have not happened before). It could be that the person recovers to live a long time, or has a temporary reprieve, or dies.

In this context, it is just as well that we have set forms of prayer to fall back on, because over the weeks, or years, specific requests will change, as the praying community adjusts to what is happening. Generalized prayer for the suffering (fine examples of which are to be found in the Alternative Service Book and the American Prayer Book) help to gather up the more specific petitions, which are not 'answered', if the person for whom prayer is made is going to die soon. The interplay of the official (general) text and the local (specific) insertion marks an important pastoral transition which the liturgy should express.

Another problem is the spiritual condition which has recently been described as the *absence of God*.[16] Many people feel this absence at different points in their lives, even in different parts of the same year, and the human sciences of psychology, psychoanalysis, and psychiatry have done much to clarify what brings on these bouts or conditions, whether they be caused by external or biochemical stress. The Church cannot turn its back on these natural phenomena among her own members, nor should they be marked off as sinful, in the way that the ancients described *accidie*, which, in our opinion, overlaps with the mental and physiological conditions which feel spiritual emptiness, and, in the case of the believing Christian, can often lead to unnecessary feelings of guilt. Some people are more prone to this than others.

Apart from an obvious concern to accompany the healing ministries of the secular world, the Christian community has a duty to proclaim the cry of dejection from the cross as an authentic part of Christian experience, and one which can (and should) find appropriate expression in public prayer. Assuming that this should not become a masochistic indulgence through undue frequency or intensity, the vital question is, how should it be expressed?

There are occasions when not just individuals but entire congregations sense the absence of God, though this will not happen frequently. When it does, the atmosphere of the celebration will probably be heavy, because of spiritual deadness, when nothing means anything, preaching seems empty, the sacraments feel lifeless. The liturgical year embodies a natural rhythm of waiting and barrenness (Advent and Lent), jubilation and splendour (Christmas and Easter), reflection and plain sailing (the 'green' Sundays). But at the heart of the personal deadness lies the intercession, which should offer up the emptiness of the community, or the individuals, as a deepening of relationship with God – for his absence implies that the relationship is there, even if it is not felt. Prayers for Church, world, suffering and departed take on a new dimension, which hymn-writers in the past have often been the only artists within the liturgy with the courage to explore, such as the Dane, Bernhard Severin Ingemann, whose manic 'Igennem nat og traengsel' is well-known in English as 'Through the night of doubt and sorrow' (even if the Martin Shaw tune is frequently still shunned in favour of the stodgy wail that deprives the hymn of much of its force!)

For many, an added difficulty arises at that stage which every Christian has to face sooner or later – *prayer and the departed*. Whether he be Catholic, Protestant, or somewhere between, bereavement will certainly make any Christian more aware of the need to express in prayer some relationship with the person who has died. As usual, the two traditional extremes offer their wares, with one side insisting on prayer *for* the departed and prayer *by* the saints, and the other side adhering to the Reformed principle of thanksgiving *only* for those who have gone before in faith.

Some find these explanations inadequate, and they are more than likely to be found so at the point of bereavement, even if the Catholic gets a thoroughly Paschal funeral, or the Protestant gets a joyful send-off. On one hand, purgatory seems unreal (and actually underplayed in modern Catholicism); on the other hand, only to give thanks locks up grief, which is so necessary. Donald Allchin has written with great perception on this question. He maintains that there is an instinct which perceives not only the world beyond at the moment of death, but a fellowship and communion of saints embracing those left behind and those who have gone before.[17] The Alexandrian Anaphora of Basil contains so much of beauty and antiquity, among which numbers a finely-phrased intercession of the departed, couched in strongly eschatological ideas, which are at once biblical, catholic, and tender:

> Since, Master, it is a command of your only-begotten Son that we should share in the commemoration of your saints, vouchsafe to remember, Lord, also those of our fathers who have been well-pleasing to you from eternity... (Then follows a list of faithful ones, and the reading of the diptychs)... Give them rest in your presence; preserve us who live here in your faith, guide us to your kingdom, and

grant us your peace at all times; through Jesus Christ and the Holy Spirit.[18]

Liturgical renewal certainly affects the style, the language, and even the attitudes to intercessory prayer. But it has gone much further than that. Comparatively little help has been given to this crucial part of Christian worship,[19] and, in consequence, we are witnessing what amounts to a creation *ex nihilo*. Through being deprived of the old and familiar, we have had to start again, and so there is set before us the opportunity to rediscover what intercession really is. Even if we have little to say, the starting-point is that intercession, isolated though it may be from other parts of the liturgy, is one of the supreme and costly privileges of the Christian.

So the tensions and the upsets and the time taken to prepare intercession – all these are hiccups that are worth while. Why? Because the real purpose of intercession is to express the essential dimensions of the Christian faith ... that we are friends of God, because we are his adopted sons and daughters ... that we are committed to each other, in a sacramental and living communion ... and that we are resolved to serve the world, and to participate in its joy and pain. The offering of intercession, therefore, should feel for these three vital sensitivities, in which language and symbol become lost in wonder, love and praise, and the liturgy becomes a mere vehicle of God's redeeming power.

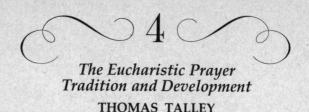

4

The Eucharistic Prayer Tradition and Development
THOMAS TALLEY

The last decade has seen significant development in the matter of the eucharistic prayer, both in our understanding of its historical evolution and in the number of such prayers employed in the liturgy. Leonel Mitchell has observed that more eucharistic anaphoras have been composed in the past ten years than in the preceding millennium.[1] This has been a somewhat surprising development in view of the long tradition attaching to the invariability of the body of the prayer. Still, the variable preface in the West has continued to remind us of the early spontaneous thanksgivings of the liturgical president in which variety of wording and specific content was framed about a more constant form or structure which served as locus of the tradition. While such freedom still has carefully drawn bounds, most liturgical reform in the West has seen fit to follow the lead of the Roman Catholic Church in introducing a number of eucharistic prayers.

Such disavowal of the presupposition that there could be but one 'canon' (the term itself was suggestive) has drawn more pointed attention to the structure behind the variety, and that, in turn, has afforded a certain practical urgency to studies in the evolution of that structure. In many instances, unfortunately, the composition of new prayers has run ahead of studies in the evolution of the form of the anaphora, but as those studies have advanced we are (however tardily) in a better position to assess the new compositions and to refine them, perhaps, in the future.

While much remains unclear in the evolution of the structure of the eucharistic prayer so that one can speak only provisionally, still the main outlines of that history seem much clearer now than they did a decade ago, so seductively as to make suspension of judgement difficult. While anything one may say today may require serious revision or abandonment tomorrow, it none the less seems appropriate at this juncture to review in general terms the state of our understanding of the anaphoral tradition, a tradition which seems to reach back to Jewish meal prayers as those were already established in the century before our era and perhaps even earlier than that.

At the outset, however, the extent of such establishment must be seriously qualified. Joseph Heinemann, in a work which throws important new light on the development of Jewish liturgy,[2] has emphasized the variety and flexibility of prayer-content and, to a lesser degree, prayer-form in the period just preceding and following the destruction of the Temple, and his findings are a welcome corrective to the tendency evident earlier in this century to treat the familiar Jewish benediction formulary (*berakah*) as the single source of the eucharistic prayer.[3] Such benediction of God is frequently encountered in Scripture, but these biblical *berakoth* are less prayers addressed to God than they are confessional praise of God phrased in the third person throughout, a late example of which can be seen in the Canticle of Zechariah (Luke 1.68ff). Heinemann argues that, like these biblical *berakoth*, the standard short *berakah* acclamation which became so central to Jewish prayer was also originally in the third person throughout. Other prayer-forms (such as thanksgivings or supplications) received short *berakoth* as their concluding 'seal' (*chatimah*), an addition to such prayers which Heinemann calls the 'eulogy'. Since these were attached to prayers already addressed to God in the second person, these concluding eulogies were also addressed to God (e.g. 'Blessed art Thou, O Lord, who buildest Jerusalem'). At a later point, the opening of the third-person *berakah* was conformed to that second-person eulogy, giving one of the characteristic features of the liturgical *berakah*, viz. an opening address to God as 'Thou' which continues to state the motive of the praise in the third person, e.g. 'Blessed art Thou, O Lord our God ..., who nourishes us and the whole world with goodness...'

While these developments probably occurred during the period of the Second Temple, one text suggests that they were quite late in that period. *The Book of Jubilees,* usually dated from the very end of the second century BC, places on the lips of Abraham such a three-part meal grace as is still standard (although a fourth prayer was added in the second century of our era). This text still shows the original forms outlined by Heinemann:[4]

1   A Benediction of God as Creator and provider of food, in the third person throughout.

2   A Thanksgiving addressed to God for his protection and sustenance, in the second person and without any concluding eulogy.

3   A Supplication for the future of the people, the sons of Abraham, again addressed to God in the second person and without any concluding eulogy.

Of this threefold prayer form, Heinemann says:

Throughout the liturgy, we find repeatedly juxtaposed the three basic and complementary motifs of Creation – Revelation (viz. the Giving of the Torah) – Redemption, which in the Rabbinic world-view mark respectively the beginning of the history of mankind, the critical turning-point in the progession of that history, and the ultimate goal and final destination of the historical continuum.[5]

The same sense of sacred history is characteristic of Christianity, but with the significant difference that the revelation of God in Christ is seen also as inauguration of redemption, while the fulfilment of that redemption at the *eschaton* remains as well the goal of our supplication. This recognition of the life, death and resurrection of Christ as not only the revelatory centre of history but also as inauguration of the Kingdom (however proleptically) makes a radical difference in the Christian sense of the shape of history, and our earliest eucharistic prayers suggest that the theme of creation was, in fact, for a time subsumed to that christocentric focus.

Leaving to one side the question of whether they framed an *agape* following the Eucharist, the prayers of *Didache* 9 and 10 manifest this christocentric focus. While the prayers in Chapter 10 follow the threefold form of the Jewish Grace after Meals, there is no Benediction of God as provider of food, but an initial

Thanksgiving for the revelation through Jesus. In the second paragraph, where one would have found such a Thanksgiving for revelation in the Jewish grace, there is a second Thanksgiving to God as creator and provider of food, but this is transformed into Thanksgiving for the spiritual food and drink given through Jesus unto eternal life. The third paragraph makes Supplication for the people as did the equivalent in the Jewish grace, but now it is for the gathering of the Church into the Kingdom. This same threefold form is found at the beginning of the Eucharist in Chapter 9. Here Thanksgivings over the cup and the broken bread replace the Benedictions of the standard meal ritual but, contrary to the usual Jewish ritual, these are followed by such a Supplication for the Church as we see in Chapter 10.

Is the displacement of Benediction-forms by Thanksgiving-forms significant, given the fact that both are popular verbs of praise which many have considered to be virtually synonymous? Two responses need to be made to that question. First, there is no question here of using a form of the Greek *eucharistein* to translate the Hebrew *baruch*. The Thanksgiving prayers of *Didache* (and in Jewish literature itself) do not follow the form of the *berakah* (which would yield, 'Thanked art Thou, O Lord our God . . .'), and are, further, in the second person throughout, unlike the *berakah* whose motive is stated in the third person. The Thanksgivings of *Didache* have parallels in Jewish prayer, but those are not to *berakoth* but to *hodayoth*, Thanksgivings addressed to God in the second person. Second, while the Greek *eucharistein* means simply thanksgiving, even in the sense of a sentiment of gratitude, the Semitic verb it translates (*yadah*) is more complex. It can mean not only to give thanks but also to confess or acknowledge, a notion which Greek renders as *exomologeomai*. How is it that the Greek *eucharistein* is so consistently chosen to render the Hebrew and Aramaic verb? While surely more remains to be said of this question, significant work has been done on the use of eucharistic language by Jews writing in Greek in the first two centuries of our era.[6] Among such writers, *eucharistein* is regularly used with *thusia* to render the Hebrew *zebach todah*, the 'sacrifice of thanksgiving' referred to in Psalm 116.15 and in many other places in the Old Testament. This was a communion-sacrifice in which part of the animal victim was consumed by fire (and so received by God) while the rest was consumed by the one who offered, sharing it with his friends, and so, symbolically, sharing a meal with God. It may also be noted that one of the ancient writers who uses *eucharistein* so consistently in a sacrificial context, Philo of Alexandria, also speaks of Passover as 'the feast of Thanksgiving'.[7]

While such semantic studies can offer no firm conclusions, we should not exclude the possibility that such sacrificial nuance played a role in shaping Christian liturgical language in connection with the rite whose sacrificial character is recognized as early as *Didache* 14. Indeed, our earliest written version of the institution-narrative, that of St Paul in 1 Corinthians 11, uses *eucharistein* to describe our Lord's prayer at the breaking of bread, while Mark (14.22) more precisely recounts that Jesus 'blessed', i.e. recited the customary *berakah*. Mark describes the historical last supper, while Paul may be understood to refer to what is already a liturgical tradition in which we show the Lord's death until he comes.

The Pauline passage shows already the beginning of the separation of the Eucharist from the complete meal which was the context of its institution. As that process continues, such a dual pattern of prayer as we have noted in *Didache* (Thanksgiving and Supplication before communion and similar prayers after, corresponding to the Grace after Meals) gave way to the single eucharistic prayer such as we see in the *Apostolic Tradition* of Hippolytus and later in an anaphora ascribed to Epiphanius of Salamis. As Louis Ligier has pointed out,[8] in both of these the prayer opens with a Christological Thanksgiving which continues to the institution narrative and its attached anamnesis. After the anamnesis, the prayer concludes with Supplication for the community, although in the prayer of Epiphanius it includes a specific invocation of the Spirit for the consecration of the gifts, a concern less precisely articulated by Hippolytus. While in both the pattern is Thanksgiving for the work of Christ and Supplication for the people as we have seen in *Didache*, that earlier document's retention of the Jewish threefold form, however amended, is surrendered in favour of one single, continuous prayer, although still bipartite in its content: Thanksgiving and Supplication.

Recently, Edward Kilmartin[9] and Geoffrey Cuming[10] have independently suggested that we might see an even earlier form of such a single prayer in what has previously been taken to be only a fragment of the anaphora of St Mark but which, they suggest, may be the whole of a very early eucharistic prayer. Contained in a papyrus at Strasbourg (gr. 254), the text is damaged at the beginning and has one major lacuna and other lesser lacunae toward the end. What is clear, however, is that it concludes, not with a transition to *Sanctus* as does its parallel in the developed liturgy of St Mark, but with such a doxology as is standard at the conclusion of prayers. Evidently opening from a eucharistic dialogue (the remaining praise verb, probably one of several, is *eulogein*), the prayer is a praise of God as Creator, through Christ, which passes into an oblation: 'with him and the Holy Spirit we give thanks to you and offer this reasonable and bloodless service . . .' This leads in turn to a Supplication for the Church and further intercession, concluding in the above mentioned doxology. There is no mention in the Strasbourg papyrus of any recitation of the institution-narrative, but it has been conjectured that it might have been read following the prayer, just before the distribution of communion. From the available evidence, however, this must remain only a conjecture.

Still, the broad variety in the wording of the narrative in the many forms in which we find it does suggest that it represents a continuing oral tradition rather than the quotation of a significant passage of Scripture, a charter narrative carried in the tradition of the liturgy, even from before its incorporation into the Gospels. It thus could well have found a place in the liturgy without being incorporated into the meal prayers which formed the core of the anaphora, and such may have been the case in *Didache* and the Alexandrian use represented by the Strasbourg papyrus.

On the other hand, recent researches in the anaphora most notorious for lacking the narrative, Addai and Mari, have suggested that the institution-narrative was not absent from the original form of the prayer, but was rather lost from it at a considerably later time.[11] Its original form, the Anaphora of the Apostles, was common source for both the Nestorian Addai and Mari and the Maronite Third Anaphora of Peter. In the latter of these the narrative occurs in the text of the Supplication, at a point where Addai and Mari betrays signs of textual emendation. The context is reminiscent of the festal embolism added to the equivalent Supplication of the Jewish meal-grace, a situation of the narrative which is in contrast to what we find in Hippolytus and West Syrian prayers. There the institution-narrative and anamnesis come at the climax of the Christological Thanksgiving, and memorial-oblation-thanks-giving are interwoven themes which articulate the Church's thank-offering of the eucharistic gifts as memorial of Christ's unique sacrifice through which we participate in the salvation accomplished by him. While fourth-century prayers of this type will reflect a trinitarian economy, already in Hippolytus the memorial-oblation of the Paschal Mystery comes to its con-clusion in the renewal of Pentecost, and the Supplication for the community asks that outpouring of the Spirit. This two-part prayer of Thanksgiving and Supplication is the nucleus from which later prayers will grow, a nucleus continuous with the (double) Thanksgiving and Supplication visible already in *Didache*.

Although the prayer in *Apostolic Tradition* opens with the familiar dialogue, it does not lead into a preface which in turn ends in *Sanctus*. Both here and in the Anaphora of Epiphanius the *Sanctus* is absent and, as Ligier has noted, the prayer is a purely christological Thanksgiving down to the institution-narrative, giving no place to the praise of the Father as Creator. Just such a praise of God as the Creator adored by the heavenly hosts, however, seems bound to the introduction of the *Sanctus* into our eucharistic prayers. The source of this praise and hymn, it has often been suggested, is the liturgy of the synagogue. The angelic hymn of Isaiah 6 (*Kedushah*) occurred at three points in the synagogue service and dispute continues as to which of these was earliest in the tradition. In any case, it is the first occurrence, at the conclusion of the first benediction before *Shema* (*Yotzer Or*), which seems to have the strongest similarities to the early Christian prayers introducing *Sanctus*. Such a source has seemed unlikely to many since the use of *Kedushah* at this point was not supported by the published Genizah fragments, but Bryan Spinks pleaded the insufficiency of that argument from silence in an essay published in 1977,[12] and in the same year there appeared the (above-mentioned) work of Heinemann, reporting studies in unpublished Genizah fragments which give support to Spinks' contention. While some have argued that the occurrence of *Sanctus* in Addai and Mari (and *a fortiori* in the Anaphora of the Apostles which was its source) represents a later intrusion into the text, this has been resisted by Macomber[13] and Spinks, although the latter has admitted recently that the appearance of *Kedushah* in the context of an anaphora based on the Grace after Meals (where *Kedushah* has never had a place) requires explanation.[14]

Until a few years ago, the earliest occurrence of *Sanctus* in the documents of the eucharistic prayer was in that which bears the name of Serapion, a text which Cuming would date around 360. However, Hans-Jörg Auf der Maur has discovered earlier reference to *Sanctus* in the Easter Homilies of Asterios Sophistes who wrote in the vicinity of Antioch probably between 335 and 341.[15] While Asterios' homilies refer to the hymn in a eucharistic context, they also point to its use in a non-eucharistic setting. We may also see such a non-eucharistic use in *Apostolic Constitutions* VII.35, and Auf der Maur points to the continuation of such use in *Te Deum*. It is easy to see the adoption of such a prayer ending in *Sanctus* from the synagogue as an element in Christian morning prayer, and the subsequent adoption of the praise of the Creator and angelic hymn as introduction to the Thanksgiving–Supplication nucleus of the anaphora, especially in East Syria where Christianity remained most strongly Jewish. Whatever the motivation for the primitive anaphora's focus on Thanksgiving, even to the extent of subsuming to it the Creation-theme of the first benediction of the meal-grace, in a strongly Semitic environment one can imagine the restoration of the original threefold pattern by the addition, from the liturgy of the daily office, of an opening Praise of the Creator hymned by the heavenly choirs.

The opening prayer in the Anaphora of the Apostles conforms to the peculiarity of the liturgical *berakah* noted above. Although the prayer (like the whole anaphora) is addressed to the Son, this begins with an address in the second person, and continues to recount the motive of the praise in the third person: 'Praise to thee, adorable and glorious Name ..., who created the world in his goodness and its inhabitants in his mercy ...'

After the prayer's conclusion in *Sanctus*, the next section begins, 'We give thanks to thee, O Lord, we thy sinful servants', and there seems no conclusive reason why we cannot look upon this Thanksgiving and the following Supplication as the original nucleus which has been restored to the threefold pattern of the Jewish meal-grace by adding a Christian adaptation of *Yotzer Or* with its *Kedushah*, a development which could well date from the third century.

While the East Syrian nucleus places the institution-narrative and anamnesis in the concluding section, the Supplication, farther west (Antioch?) a nucleus such as we have seen in Hippolytus, where the narrative and anamnesis conclude the Thanksgiving, seems to have adopted a similar Praise of the Creator leading into *Sanctus.* Connected to this hymn in the extant prayers by reiteration of 'Holy', there follows a christological Thanksgiving (including narrative and anamnesis) and a Supplication which opens with a consecratory epiclesis of the Spirit. While this tripartite anaphoral form is commonly designated 'Antiochene', since the fourth century such forms have spread far from West Syria and have had significant impact on other traditions down to our own day.

One area where it is interesting to find such an anaphora is in the Coptic Church. There an anaphora bearing the name of St Basil is today the standard eucharistic prayer and, while considerably shorter, it is closely related to the more prolix Byzantine anaphora which bears the same name. Evidently introduced to Alexandria from Cappadocia (by Basil?) in the fourth century, it early shared the attention of the Alexandrian Church with other prayers, one of which (represented by the previously discussed Strasbourg papyrus) emerged as the most common Egyptian anaphora of the medieval period, the Anaphora of St Mark (more recently St Cyril).

It is tempting to speculate that the prayer's unusual features are the result of the influence of the early form of Basil on such a primitive nucleus as we find in the Strasbourg papyrus. This was the concern of Geoffrey Cuming in a major paper presented at the Oxford Patristic Conference in 1979.[16] Such a Praise of the Creator ending in *Sanctus* as characterizes the early text of Basil would ill suit the old Alexandrian nucleus, since creation was already its theme. Therefore, *Sanctus* in Alexandria was appended to the end of the original nucleus, a suitable transition replacing the doxology. The nucleus, however, had already made the transition from Thanksgiving to Supplication, and it was in the supplicatory mode, therefore, that the prayer continued after *Sanctus*, building a connection with this hymn through an opening petition that God will *fill* the sacrifice (already offered in the original nucleus) with his blessing, as heaven and earth are *full* of his glory. This leads, in St Mark, to the institution-narrative, anamnesis (its oblation now in the past tense), and consecratory epiclesis. However, in two Egyptian fragments (one of them no longer extant) the petition immediately following *Sanctus* is itself a consecratory epiclesis. While defects in these fragments make it impossible to know the full contents of the later epiclesis following the anamnesis, appeal has been made to them as evidence for an Alexandrian tradition which divided the epiclesis so as to place supplication for consecration of the gifts before the institution-narrative and for the Communicants after the anamnesis; such is the scheme now found in the eucharistic prayers of the Roman Missal and the Alternative Service Book of the Church of England. Careful reading of the liturgical evidence for such a division of concerns of the epiclesis has suggested to several writers that it reflects a theological presupposition rather than any significant Alexandrian tradition.[17]

The evolution of the eucharistic prayer at Rome is still far from clear, though its close relationship to the tradition of northern Italy represented by the *De Sacramentis* of Ambrose seems to be firmly established. Ambrose is concerned to explain what is presented as if it were a rather fixed text, although he refers as well to earlier parts ('praise is offered to God, prayer is made for the people, for kings, for others') where the words are described as those of the priest. These more variable Thanksgivings and Supplications have survived in a few cases, and we have two examples of them quoted by an anonymous Arian of about Ambrose's time. The second of these fragments, first edited by Mai, shows us a Thanksgiving which proceeds from the customary introductory dialogue and then moves into a Supplication which includes oblation of the sacrifice. Neither in this fragment nor in *De Sacramentis* do we find any reference to

Sanctus, but it must have entered the tradition of Rome well before 530, around which date the author of *Liber Pontificalis* ascribed its introduction to Sixtus I in the second century. When it did enter the Roman tradition it formed the conclusion of a Thanksgiving which was variable and probably composed for each occasion, and was followed by the relatively invariable Supplications which we know as the *Canon Missae*, the seeds of which are seen in *De Sacramentis*, although the earliest documentary evidence for the standard text is more than three centuries later than that fourth-century work.

At some point in this period (probably earlier rather than later) the prayer before the institution-narrative – the parallel to which in *De Sacramentis* prayed God to make the oblation acceptable, 'because it is the figure of the body and blood of our Lord' – has become a petition for the consecration of the gifts which asks God to make the offering acceptable, 'that it may become to us the body and blood of your dearly beloved Son Jesus Christ our Lord.' While the petition does not identify any moment of consecration, appeal to it and to Ambrose's emphasis on the words of Christ gave rise to the Western (and particularly scholastic) theological tradition which identified the transformation of the gifts with the recital of the *verba Christi*, a development which cast what follows in the prayer into considerable ambiguity. The anamnesis, *Unde et memores*, makes oblation of 'the holy bread of eternal life and the cup of everlasting salvation', classical language for such a prayer which, however, seems inappropriately modest if one has already come to identify those gifts as the very body and blood of Christ. The following prayers (*Supra quae* and *Supplices te rogamus*) are similarly difficult to relate to such a theology of consecration, and Nicholas Cabasilas considered *Supplices* to be the Roman equivalent of the Byzantine consecratory epiclesis (as, indeed, did Louis Duchesne).[18] However, if one identifies the *verba Christi* as a 'moment of consecration', the oblation in the following anamnesis becomes problematic even beyond its classically modest expression. St Thomas Aquinas, in a seldom cited text, seems to flinch from the implication that in *Unde et memores* the body and blood of Christ are offered to the Father. In accord with previous liturgical tradition, he sees the consecration of the gifts as *consequent upon* their oblation as the sacrifice of the Church, even though he is already bound to the theology which situates that consecration in the institution-narrative. In *Summa Theologica* III (Q.83.a.4), Thomas describes the rite of the Mass:

> So, then, after the people have been prepared and instructed, the next step is to proceed to the celebration of the mystery, which is both offered as a sacrifice, and consecrated and received as a sacrament: since first we have the oblation; then the consecration of the matter offered; and thirdly its reception.

The oblation to which he refers, of course, is the 'offertory', consisting in his description of the offertory chant and the *oratio super oblata*. Of the classical *offerimus* in the anamnesis, *Unde et memores*, he makes no mention at all, and says of the prayer only that in it the priest 'makes excuse for his presumption in obeying Christ's command, saying, *Unde et memores, etc.*' Thomas clings to an understanding of the relation of oblation and consecration which is visible in all previous liturgical tradition, even though the current theology of consecration forced him to disregard the role and even the text of the anamnesis.

The anamnesis following the institution-narrative is, in Hippolytus and in the Byzantine tradition, always set within the Thanksgiving for the work of Christ and is followed by a Supplication, one of the concerns of which is prayer for the consecration of the gifts, yielding that liturgical syntax, oblation → consecration, which Thomas transposed. Where, as in Roman tradition, Thanksgiving is limited to the variable preface, and the institution-narrative and anamnesis fall within the extended Supplication, it is more easy, perhaps, to lose sight of the classical relation of these concerns to one another. Still, the Anaphora of the Apostles in its Maronite form (Peter III) does situate the narrative and anamnesis within such a Supplication and yet (probably from the fourth century) adds its epiclesis following the anamnesis and reiterated oblation.

Modern liturgical theology has long since wearied of quests for a 'moment of consecration', and most today would point to the total anaphora as consecratory. This is surely a laudable approach, but it does not free us from the responsibility of attending critically to the relation of the themes of eucharistic sacrifice and consecration in liturgical tradition and in theological commentary, however complex that may be.[19] Even if oblation and consecration be considered to be rigorously reciprocal, such reciprocity is difficult to express in the prayers themselves, and any liturgical suggestion that the order of these concerns is consecration → oblation is likely to confront us afresh with such theological polarization as sixteenth-century Europe witnessed. While one may not oversimplify the conflict over eucharistic sacrifice in that troubled time, it seems fair to say that it focused in large part, if not primarily, on the rightness or wrongness of the Church's oblation of the sacramental body and blood of Christ. Unlike St Thomas, Catholic theologians of that time seem quite comfortable with the notion that consecration makes significant oblation possible, while reformers recoiled from such a theology of eucharistic sacrifice to the extent of removing any suggestion of a memorial-oblation of the gifts (and, indeed, any notion of oblation of bread and wine even at the offertory). In spite of the truly great advances in our understanding of the anaphora in the present century, that difference regarding the anamnesis seems still to contrast the Roman and English prayers.

A particularly painful example of this inversion of concerns is Eucharistic Prayer IV of the Missal of Paul VI. This anaphora took as its starting point the Coptic Anaphora of Basil discussed above, a tripartite prayer of the West Syrian type where institution-narrative and anamnesis brought a christological Thanksgiving to its climax and, through a transitional popular acclamation, gave way to the Supplication which opened with the consecratory epiclesis. In the Roman recasting of this prayer, however, a supplicatory epiclesis for the consecration of the gifts has been inserted prior to the institution-narrative, interrupting the Thanksgiving, and the following anamnesis now makes an unprecedented oblation of 'his body and blood, the acceptable sacrifice which brings salvation to the whole world'. Of that oblation, Father Aidan Kavanagh has written:

> This is novel, and can hardly be said to retain 'a most definitely traditional character'. One who has some acquaintance with the medieval and reformation history of eucharistic

controversy will recognize the inadequacy of such a position, and may be forgiven his disappointment that its tendentiousness has got into a Catholic formulary precisely at a time when it could have been diagnosed and avoided most easily.[20]

The other new Roman prayers retain more classical language of oblation in the anamnesis, but since these, too, are preceded by a consecratory epiclesis, one is left with the impression that Prayer IV is theologically normative, and that those more classical expressions are to be understood in the sense made explicit in Prayer IV.

However ill-founded the claims to a tradition of such a divided epiclesis at Alexandria, it is understandable that fidelity to conciliar authority in the Roman Church raises problems for prayer for the consecration of the gifts following the institution-narrative (although Catholics of Byzantine and other oriental rites in communion with Rome do so regularly). It is less easy for an American Anglican to understand why the Church of England has elected such a division of the epiclesis for its current reforms. While general rejoicing must greet the reintegration of the eucharistic prayer in the Alternative Service Book, it would be less than even-handed, in the light of what has been said above, to neglect to comment on the effect of such a consecratory epiclesis prior to the narrative, and especially in the Third Eucharistic Prayer, based as it is on Hippolytus. The supplicatory epiclesis interrupts the Thanksgiving within which Hippolytus situated the narrative and anamnesis in a way directly analogous to the Roman distortion of the Coptic Basil.

Unlike Prayer IV, however, no English anamnesis is in danger of making oblation of 'his body and blood'. Quite to the contrary, having made that Supplication for the consecration of the gifts, all the new English prayers (as did 1549) find themselves indisposed to make unambiguous oblation of them in the anamnesis at all. The recent American revision also attempted such a pre-narrative epiclesis in one eucharistic prayer (Rite II, Eucharistic Prayer C), and encountered the same difficulty in the anamnesis. While such diffidence is surely preferable to the oblation of 'his body and blood', we might wonder at the value of an anaphoral structure which seems to force such a choice upon us. Is a preliminary consecratory epiclesis worth the agony that has surrounded all our attempts to frame a generally satisfying anamnesis which would take account not only of the evidence of the tradition but also the concern of the reformers (and of Thomas Aquinas!) to avoid oblation of Christ's sacramental body and blood? An outsider may be allowed to pose this question only if he remembers that response to it will surely involve issues and concerns which are not his own. One formed in an anaphoral tradition whose final shape owed much to Thomas Rattray's eighteenth-century studies in the Liturgy of St James may easily be rendered myopic by West Syrian-Scottish-American chauvinism; but it is tempting to wonder whether such diffidence over oblation of the gifts in the anamnesis would still be characteristic of the eucharistic prayer in the Church of England had the Alternative Order of the Proposed Book of Common Prayer outlived the débâcle of 1928. One may at least be allowed to hope that the structure of that prayer has not been forgotten for ever in the Church of England.

A particularly welcome initiative of the Liturgical Commission of the General Synod in its revision of Series 3 was the removal of the acclamation, 'Christ has died, etc.,' to a position following the anamnesis, but the initiative in GS 364 failed in GS 364A the following year, and the acclamation once again divides the narrative from the anamnesis as it does in all Roman prayers, in two of the American prayers, and in recent revision fairly generally. The acclamation, which comes from the Liturgy of St James in Malabar (*via* Ratcliff's liturgy for Bombay and The Book of Common Worship of the Church of South India), has become something of a *sine qua non* of contemporary eucharistic prayers, a fashion which seems, again, to have developed just in advance of studies in anaphoral structure which might have discouraged it had they appeared a decade earlier. There is such an acclamation in St James and in the Indian prayers derived from it, but in all those there is still another popular acclamation following the anamnesis, marking the major transition from the christological Thanksgiving to the pneumatological Supplication. The broad Western adoption of this one acclamation out of that tradition is unfortunate in that it divides the narrative from the anamnesis and interrupts the significant traditional continuity between them, a continuity which, as noted above, Ligier regards as original. At the same time, when (with *Sanctus* and the final *Amen*) it constitutes one of three congregational responses, it gives the impression of recreating a threefold structure in the anaphora, but one which does not correspond to the trinitarian pattern which is still visible in the classical oriental anaphoras. Indeed, it is fascinating to note that, in spite of the fairly general concern to restore creation to the anaphora, and the desire of almost every tradition to have at least one eucharistic prayer based on Hippolytus, no recent reform with which I am familiar has sought to reintroduce what the tradition seems to have done, namely to prefix a Praise of the Creator concluding in *Sanctus* to a nucleus consisting of Thanksgiving and Supplication such as we find in the *Apostolic Tradition* just as it is. A prayer with just that trinitarian structure, 'A Common Eucharistic Prayer' composed by an ecumenical group and derived from the Coptic version of Basil, has been adopted in the American Book of Common Prayer of 1979 (Rite II, Eucharistic Prayer D), and is a gratifying example of liturgiological impact on liturgical reform.[21]

Its trinitarian pattern is due to no theologically dictated invention, but is a pattern of prayer already visible in Jewish liturgy before the Christian era, as Heinemann observed (though in different terms). One could, indeed, make a strong case for the suggestion that it is liturgical structure which provided the framework for the theological reflection which emerged as the doctrine of the Holy Trinity. Praise of the Creator hymned in heaven – Thanksgiving for Revelation and Redemption in Christ – Supplication for the Spirit's renewal of the community and its mission: such is the pattern which, at the very least, developed in the liturgy in reciprocity with the theological reflection, feeding it and fed by it.

Alongside the trinitarian pattern, of course, there were others which remained more bipartite, as at Alexandria and Rome, and these expanded the concerns and contents of the Supplication following *Sanctus*, adding there the institution-narrative and anamnesis. In our Western theology and spirituality, Supplication tended to be reduced to a 'Prayer of Consecration', a development which seriously limited the depth and scope of the classical eucharistic prayer. As we turn from such an oversimplification today, we could perhaps do worse than to brood deeply and lovingly over the total history and character of this central prayer of the Church's kerygmatic enactment of her understanding of herself and of her Lord. This might take us beyond piecemeal repairs to our immediate past, preserve us from novelties which thinly mask the intransigence of questionable if not discredited presuppositions, and lead to further reforms which would be authentically traditional, truly radical and, therefore, broadly ecumenical. *Legem credendi*, after all, *lex statuat supplicandi.*

5

Shape and Liturgy
DAVID TRIPP

Significant Form

In his superb science-fiction novel *The Black Cloud*, the astronomer Fred Hoyle asks us to imagine a vast mass of gas, charged with electrical activity that turns out to be intelligence, visiting our solar system to gather stocks of energy from our sun so that it can continue an urgent voyage across the universe. Professor Hoyle's counterparts in the story have the presence of mind to try to make contact with the cloud by radio – no great problem, for the cloud houses an intelligence that can easily recognize and analyse anything so obviously patterned as a language, even on our barbaric level. The cloud is very surprised, for, in its wide experience, intelligence is normally possible only in large and diffuse bodies like itself, and the appearance of rationality in anything so crude as our all too solid flesh is a turn-up for the cosmic books. None the less, the cloud is not very impressed, and treats the humans with a tolerant patience and condescension, until the scientists of earth stop spelling out their ignorance of physics, and play a symphony of Beethoven. Then, and only then, the cloud finds evidence of reason in *homo sapiens (sapiens!)*. It has to point out, however, that we play Beethoven too slowly . . .

Here, as in all his works of fiction, Hoyle is entertaining us with ideas that in themselves can and should be taken seriously. In this story, the possibilities of communication between greatly differing life-forms by the mediation of significant form are aired too briefly for adequate discussion, but the author draws attention to a discussion for which materials are already plentifully available: in modern study of language, in the decipherment of ancient scripts like Linear B, in recent advances in formal and informal logics, aesthetics and politics – all are concerned with form, with structure.

In aesthetics, the subject of form in art can be contentious to the point of absurdity (who can now read T. W. H. Crosland's chapter on 'Sonnet Legislation', in his *The English Sonnet* of 1917, without choking with laughter?); but the need for form in human expression, in human mentation, in human relationships, is real enough, as the still unfinished work of the Gestalt psychologists testifies.

Significant form has always at least two dimensions: the existential and the sequential. The existential is the shape and meaning of this moment, of this present experience and configuration of relationships; the sequential is the shape and meaning given to life by past and future. In the visual arts, for example, the two aspects can be considered quite independently. For example: Bill Brandt's photography has moved from essentially naturalistic studies in the Camden Town to work in the 1970s so abstract that his nude models merge into the forms of his favoured beach-scenes, even to the point of losing their immediately recognizable humanity. The sequence of styles is a significant development; but each period (and indeed each photograph from each period), has the right to be appreciated in terms of its own form and method, without being forced on to a Procrustean bed of comparison with earlier or later work. In other areas, however, sequence is crucial, as in the narrative arts. 'The story is primitive,' says E. M. Forster[1], 'it reaches back to the origins of literature, before reading was discovered, and it appeals to what is primitive in us.' But Forster is only partly correct, for the appeal of the story is also to our capacity for the future, for growth, for hope.

It is not an accident that one of our time's leading liturgists is also a musicologist, a historian and a pastor. For the maker, the student, the user, the expositor of liturgy, significant form is a necessity of life, for both existential and sequential form are essential factors in the strategy of revelation.

Shape and Interpretation

In liturgy, the role of significant form is neither simple nor always comforting. There have been times of reformation or reconstruction when the shaping of liturgies has been a matter of conscious policy. There have been other times when liturgical change has taken place by instinct, sometimes very untidily, sometimes with a consistency that appears only to a later eye. For the most part, Anton Baumstark's 'laws' of liturgical development, so fascinatingly unravelled in his pioneering book *Liturgie comparée*, have been 'obeyed' rather as lemmings obey whatever laws they do obey. There is in any case no way of predicting whether a liturgy constructed by thought and skill will prove to be better than one that has simply happened.

To add to this happy confusion, we must note that worshippers will find (or impose) significant form in their experience of liturgy which may bear little relation to what, if anything, the framers of their tradition thought they were doing. Here are three very different examples of such a process.

Cranmer's Eucharist of 1552 is essentially a Bucerian rite, but most of the tradition which has fed on it has survived by giving it a markedly non-Bucerian and non-Cranmerian interpretation. Like Bucer (who also influenced Calvin and through him Knox), Cranmer seeks to obey the command to 'do this' by giving thanks. For him, thanksgiving in the present state of things is inseparably intertwined with penitence, because thanksgiving is for the salvation that sin made necessary. The heart of his rite is thanksgiving: 'Derely beloued in the Lord . . . repent you truely . . . And aboue all thynges, ye muste geue most humble and hartie thankes to God the father, the sonne, and the holy ghost, for the redemption of the worlde... You that doe trule and earnestly repent you... Drawe near...' And then through the General Confession + Absolution + Comfortable Words into 'Lyfte up your heartes . . . glory be to thee, O lord, most high'. Then, the Thanksgiving finished – yes, *finished*, and the change is marked by the celebrant kneeling down – the communion is introduced by two prayers for fruitful reception: 'We doe not presume...', and 'Almighty God oure heauenly father...'

For the Caroline divines, of course, this was too far from Western Catholic tradition; but the rite as Cranmer left it was patient of reinterpretation and in due course received it. 'Dearly beloved in the Lord...' to Comfortable Words was given a new status as a penitential interlude; and 'Lift up your hearts...' + Preface-and-Sanctus + Humble Access + the now renamed

'Prayer of Consecration' could be seen as a version, eccentric but recognizably authentic, of the Western type of Canon. This Caroline reinterpretation carried even John Wesley along. In his 1784 *Sunday Service*, the 'third exhortation' has simply vanished, leaving only 'Ye that do truly . . .' (and, when pressed, Wesley was prepared to begin the Communion at Humble Access!). Although the Wesleyan revisers of 1882 restored the third exhortation, the Caroline reinterpretation survived; and High Church Methodists of the 1960s were putting a hymn between Comfortable Words and the Dialogue to separate Dialogue + Preface + Sanctus + Humble Access + Consecration and to let it stand apart as a Canon. Debates on this topic, even when supposedly historical in character,[2] show how liturgists confuse the notions of what they feel ought to have happened with the probabilities of history.

The tradition of liturgical commentary in the East offers another helpful example. The intense preoccupation of 'Dionysius the Areopagite' with hierarchies of orders of being, and with the penetration of these successive orders by the divine light, could easily have made all Eastern traditions of liturgical commentary indifferent to the concrete order and content of the liturgy. It is therefore all the more interesting to see how close to the observable sequence of the liturgy two important commentators, both influenced by the *Hierarchies*, still contrived to keep. Yet even in their cases, a process of reinterpretation has begun.

The eighth-century bishop George 'of the Arabs' expects his hearers to follow the liturgy closely, and to find in its sequence the pattern of the faith. His exposition is however somewhat hampered by a love of typological interpretation of static elements; and at the crucial moment of the Anaphora, we take leave of the liturgical sequences altogether, and all that we are aware of is the threefold role of the priest (as a likeness of our Redeemer, as the tongue in the head of the ecclesiastical body, and as portraying spiritual images by a mystery). Clearly, the Anaphora is no longer the direct concern of the laity, for whom George is writing. By contrast, the *Explanation of the Mysteries of the Oblation* of the ninth-century bishop Moses bār Kēphā goes back to a detailed comment on every phrase of the rite, the Anaphora included; but note that his book is intended for the clergy, and specifically for celebrants.[3]

Five hundred years later, Nicholas Cabasilas is still following the liturgy closely – but the influence of the all-pervasive diaconal litanies, intruding between the laity and the essential action beyond the ikonostas, may be seen in the fact that he has placed his general account of the significance of the sacrifice at the start of his exposition of the psalmody. Already mentioned here, however, are secondary interpretations – the little entrance as symbolic of the Epiphany, the great entrance as symbolic of Christ's self-manifestation to his enemies on Palm Sunday – which in *The Divine Liturgy of the Russian Orthodox Church* by Nikolai Gogol (1809–51) have such prominence that the imported symbolism of Christ's life, death and burial dominate the scene, and obscure the inherent shape of the rite.[4]

St Paul's exposition of the Lord's Supper illustrates how, at one and the same time, the same person can interpret the sequence for one and the same rite in terms of two quite distinct patterns.

In 1 Corinthians 10, Paul is using the Eucharist as a reminder of the commitment of the Christian to Christ, and of the consequent cost of alienation from the surrounding pagan world. In the course of this argument (10.6–30), he sums up the eucharistic action thus: 'The cup of blessing which we bless, is it not a participation in the blood of Christ? The bread which we break, is it not a participation in the body of Christ?' (v.16). Verse 17 – 'Because there is one bread, we who are many are one body, for we all partake of the one bread' – is a digression at this point, for the exposition of the Eucharist as fellowship belongs to the coming stage of his argument, and only comes in here because of Paul's associations with the term 'body', which comes into its own in Chapter 11. In Chapter 10, he is concerned with the similarity and the contrast between the Christian Eucharist and the sacrifices of Jews and pagans. For Paul, the sequence 'cup–bread' suggests the idea of offering, of sacrifice, and of the associated communion with the one who is worshipped. There is a similarity here, of course, with the sequence found in the shorter (and beyond doubt original) text of Luke 22.14–23.

1 Corinthians 11.17–34[a] appeals to the Eucharist, but now as to a model of communion among the co-worshippers. For this purpose (and we must not read back into Paul the modern

jargonistic dichotomy of 'vertical'/'horizontal' 'dimensions'!) Paul picks out the sequence 'bread–cup'. Since this sequence calls to mind Paul's own narrative (11.23–6), it is almost unquestionably the version used by Paul in teaching (and in prayer?).

But what, we still have to ask, was the liturgical sequence which Paul followed in the Eucharist? Can it possibly have been cup–bread? Was it not rather usually bread–cup, but in the knowledge that our Lord himself had left the memory of a cup–bread–cup sequence? And, if the latter obtained, was perhaps the cup–bread sequence re-enacted at a baptismal Eucharist, when sharing in the benefits of Christ's sacrifice was the dominant theme? Yet, whatever ritual pattern Paul knew and used, his combination of two 'trajectories' of exposition through the same data reminds us that we are not tied to one uniform pattern, whether in liturgical action or in spiritual apprehension.

The Shape of Liturgy Encapsulated: The Eucharistic Prayer

During his debate with Heracleides[5], Origen discussed the relation between the Father's deity and the deity of Christ. At this point, he had to turn aside to discuss a feature of the Church's liturgy which embarrassed his case – just as the 'Arian Prefaces', which were of course *Catholic* prayers quoted by an Arian author, served to embarrass the Catholic case in the West. He refers to the frequency of demands for tests of orthodoxy: bishops, and those of their clergy suspected of deviation, are presented with a credal formula imposed by authority, for their signature. With some diffidence, deferring to the authority of God and also of the bishops, but further to that of presbyters and people, Origen suggests a more lasting and effective safeguard for sound doctrine. At present, he observes:

> the Anaphora is addressed to God Almighty 'through Jesus Christ', as if confining to the Father the divinity which also belongs to the Son. No one, of course, wants to say the Anaphora twice [presumably, to the Father and then to the Son]; but let it be addressed to God 'through God' [sc., when Christ is named as mediator, he should also be given the title of divinity]. Shall I seem impertinent in suggesting the

adoption of such customs in prayer? If not, then 'Look not on his countenance, nor on the height of his stature'. Is such an one a bishop, occupying the lime-light? Even so – if he does not do as I suggest, and observe these usages, he is giving rise to new disputes: if a bishop or a presbyter, he is no true bishop or presbyter, nor yet a lay member; if a deacon, he is no true deacon, nor yet a lay member; if a lay member, he is no true lay member, nor does he have any part in the congregation. If you agree, let these usages be established.

There is not a scrap of evidence that Origen's suggestion was taken up, within his own Church of Egypt or in any other (and in his own land, any association with his name of any suggestion would before long have ensured its condemnation). Certain other changes took place to avoid giving countenance in Catholic worship to Arian interpretations, but this adaptation was not one of them. In any case, the force of tradition was too great for so abrupt a development at this stage. Yet Origen's instinct was right so far: the Eucharistic Prayer is the heart of the liturgy, and there, above all, the essential shape of worship, reflecting the proportion of the Faith, must be observed.

That shape is thanksgiving. Although in the detailed study of the Last Supper we may have to allow for the distinction between 'thanksgiving' and 'blessing', they resolve essentially into one; and the universal tradition of Christian language has been to characterize the chief prayer at the Church's chief act of worship as 'The Thanksgiving', whatever titles or contents it may have gathered to itself.

Even that point of agreement is less simple than might be expected. The late Edward Ratcliff based much of his research into the early history of the Anaphora on the view that there should have existed, if only at the very dawn of Christian liturgical history, a 'pure eucharistia', a prayer – perhaps, better, a hymn – solely of thanksgiving. To such a scheme, any petition (e.g. an embryonic epiclesis) would have to be a later addition. His views had some influence on Anglican liturgical revision; but, for him no less than for Origen, the force of tradition was too strong. On reflection, and in due loyalty to Ratcliff's own scientific standards, one must say that tradition was right.

The very nature of thanksgiving supposes a grateful

dependence that delights to ask that which the one thanked delights to give; this gift in turn evokes renewed thankfulness – and so forth in a ceaseless interchange of love. This has been seen as the ground-plan of all Christian prayer and life. In *Stromateis* VII.xii, Clement of Alexandria offers us this scheme of prayer:

(*a*) reception of the knowledge of God, acknowledged in thanksgiving for past, present and future blessings;

(*b*) prayer for spiritual enlightenment, both of oneself and of others (this element of intercession involved the advanced Christian in sharing responsibility for the faults of his brethren – a vital mark of the Catholic 'Gnostic');

(*c*) praise, which never really stops, rounds the prayer off.

Certainly, this pattern is seen clearly in several classic Christian prayers, such as that of Polycarp in his *Acts*. It appears also in Jewish prayers; and when one comes across it yet again in pagan devotion (as in some Hermetic prayers, or in the Hymn of Cleanthes), one is given seriously to think. Our schema looks as if it may be of the essence of all revelation.

Under the concept of thanksgiving may be subsumed all the apparently irreconcilable notions put forward as rival criteria for the purpose and style of the Eucharistic Prayer:

We give thanks in response to the all-encompassing vocative of divine love: thanksgiving is obedience.

We give thanks because, on one particular day, in one particular room, one man did this before he went to one particular garden, on his way to one unique tree: thanksgiving is remembrance.

As we give thanks, we share with God what is his own eternally and what is always being given to us: thanksgiving is oblation.

As we give thanks, we open ourselves in trustful dependence to God who wishes to give us what he is through what he has made: thanksgiving is invocation.

To give thanks is to allow God to bridge the gap which

disobedience has made of time and space and matter: thanksgiving is communion.

To give thanks is to know forgiveness.

To give thanks is to know already the perfect courtesy of the Lamb at the banquet in the last and everlasting day.

To give thanks is to accept a share in the Father's responsibility for all his children: it implies intercession.

It also enters into the Son's unity in the Spirit with the Father: it implies Trinitarian mysticism.

Thanksgiving is for God being God, *propter magnam gloriam*: it is adoration.

The sequence of these elements within any given Eucharistic Prayer may rightly vary. The Institution-Narrative has been variously placed: (a) before the Thanksgiving, as Christ's command, so that the following Thanksgiving is clearly obedience in the power of the Spirit; (b) as summary or recapitulation of the Trinitarian Thanksgiving, as being itself part of God's mighty acts; (c) before the epiclesis, as specifying the intention of our invocation; (d) in the petition for fruitful reception, as prayer for the Presence; or even (e) between the Thanksgiving and the communion, as if it were a divine pledge of Christ's word being realized, and that here and now.[6] This is but one example.

Unless it is proved otherwise, we should expect to be able to traverse the themes of the Prayer by different trajectories, for they belong together within the unity of the Faith which reflects that within the God we worship. The principle of *Quicunque vult* applies here: 'none before, and none after'. So far, no church in modern times, even those which offer alternative Eucharistic Prayers, has tried to include all the main possibilities within its stock of liturgical material. Why not?

The Shape of the Setting of the Eucharistic Prayer

Gregory Dix's name will be for ever linked with the observation of the change from the shape of the Last Supper to that of the emergent Eucharist, from what he called the 'Seven-Action

73

Shape' (Taking of bread – thanksgiving for bread – eating – taking of cup – thanksgiving for cup – drinking) to what he taught us all to call 'The Four-Action Shape' (Taking of bread and cup – thanksgiving for bread and cup – breaking of bread – eating and drinking).

We may feel that the 'Seven-Action Shape' (which certainly appears in Paul, Mark and Matthew) is itself a simplification of a longer pattern implied by the confusing text of Luke. The question of the Lucan account is of crucial importance to dogmatic theology, and less directly to liturgy; but we must pause to discuss it.

Behind Luke 22.14–19[a] lies an account of the Last Supper as a Passover ('*this* Passover', he said, v.15, pointing at the Passover lamb before them on the table, cf. v.13). During the opening Kiddush, Jesus says the usual grace over the cup, and then announces that he is not sharing the Passover meal; nor will he drink wine until his vow to the Father is fulfilled and the Kingdom inaugurated. He is stepping outside the covenanted protection pledged by the Passover; he is moving out of the Father's protecting ambience into the 'strange and dreadful strife, When Death and Life contended'. This vow of abstinence is reflected in Mark 14.25 and its derivative in Matthew 26.29, but transferred to the second cup. Some have been convinced that Luke knew only a cup–bread Last Supper and Eucharist, but Vööbus' work[7] has shown how for Luke the 'bread' is metonymous for bread + cup. Although the long text of Luke 22.19[b]–20 is most certainly an interpolation, the result is that the longer text of Luke gives the fullest account of the events of Maundy Thursday. There is no evidence – except, very improbably, 1 Corinthians 10 – that our Lord's abstinence was re-enacted in Christian liturgy. How could it be? This was the unique aspect of the Last Supper, that could not be reduplicated, and could indeed hardly be described at all. It was the moment when a life of devotion to the Father's will came to its climax in accepting the coming death, so turning the disaster into a sacrifice. What this means for the doctrine of the atonement can be seen from the exponents of the 'sacrificial' theory (J. S. Lidgett, N. Hicks, V. Taylor); and it is at this point that the conflict about the eucharistic sacrifice ought to find its solution, and the pioneers here are Sir Will Spens and Maurice de la Taille (and Lidgett should be mentioned here as well). It is only in the light of Jesus' abstinence that the following words and actions can be understood, for it was this that gave them a meaning that justifies and requires them to be repeated through the years. This was not a repeatable liturgical act, as they became – and liturgy is our concern here.

And so to the 'Taking', which (says Dix) survived into the 'Four-Action Shape'. It has been made a peg on which to hang the Offertory, the 'Laying of the Table', the 'Setting Apart'; but this is too much weight for the gesture in the Institution Narrative to bear. These later features need to be justified on other grounds (and they can be), but they have no sanction in the Last Supper. The only scriptural warrant for them is found in Oecolampadius' *Testament des Herrn*. To accommodate the Offertory or its reformed like into the liturgical action, his Institution-Narrative includes the whole account of the disciples sent to prepare the Passover!

More importantly, any reading of the Last Supper narratives in the light of Jewish practice forbids us to separate 'Taking' from 'Thanking'. The Bread-Thanksgiving of the Last Supper must have been after the Commemoration of the Exodus and before the Eating of the Bitter Herbs:

> The master of the house takes the two whole cakes and the broken one [broken after the opening Kiddush, in silence] in his hand together; and breaks the upper cake. But do not eat of it, till he breaks a piece of the already broken one and says the following Blessing, gives a piece of each to every one at table, who says the same Blessing, and then eat both pieces together:

> 'Blessed art thou, O Lord our God, King of the Universe, who bringest forth bread from the earth'.

> And after this, the usual *Motzi* before a meal, [the special Berakah for the Days of Unleavened Bread.]

> 'Blessed art thou, O Lord, our God, King of the Universe, who hast sanctified us with thy commandments and commanded us to eat unleavened cakes.'[8]

Picking up the bread and holding it is part of the act of thanksgiving – specifying that for which thanks is offered.

The case of the cup is less clear. In modern Jewish prayer, the cup is held for the same reason by the one who leads grace. Although the rubrics do not say that the cup is held throughout *Birkat ha-Mazon*, the Last Supper narratives suggest that this was so. 'Taking' and 'Thanking' cannot be separated.

English Anglican Rite A, 1980, so far acknowledges this insight by distinguishing the Offertory emphatically from the 'Taking', but it still requires the president to pick up the bread and cup – and put them down again!! – before the Eucharistic Prayer.

What of the Fraction? In the Passover rite as handed down, the principal Fraction precedes the saying of the appropriate *Berakah*. It has been suggested by Christians learned in Jewish devotion that at the Last Supper the bread was broken as the bread-thanksgiving began;[9] but the New Testament accounts agree unanimously that Jesus broke bread *after* the prayer (the verb for the prayer being in the aorist participial form, all the variant readings included). The clear association of the Fraction, in all the accounts, with the revolutionary words, ' . . . This is my body . . .' must indicate that the gesture was out of the ordinary. Whether or not Jesus broke the bread before the Grace, he certainly went out of his way to break it afterwards, and the likelihood is that, for this considered prophetic act, he postponed the breaking until the prayer was finished.

The most attractive interpretation of such a change in the ritual sequence is that of Rudolf Otto,[10] that the Fraction was a prophecy of the passion, expected by Jesus to be a stoning; but this exegesis is incomplete without the added realization that the fraction kept still something of its existing meaning as 'breaking-for-sharing': 'He meant their action to be a means whereby they might share in the power of His self-offering and the virtue of His approaching death' (so Vincent Taylor on Mark 14.22). Thus also the Fraction, the Eating and the Drinking are made repeatable actions: they do not belong, as the abstinence of Jesus does, in the privacy of the Son with his Father.

Before the Fraction, the Christian ecclesia could not long content itself with a Jewish grace for bread, for all its pure and devout simplicity; and it was only to be expected that the bread-thanksgiving gathered into itself the fullness of the concluding cup-thanksgiving (cf. *Didache* 10) and soon became *the*

Thanksgiving.

The second cup was graced with no gesture like the Fraction. It was only a matter of time until that was provided, in Baxter's *Savoy Liturgy* of 1661, where the pouring of consecrated wine into the various chalices needed for a Puritan Lord's Supper was made a symbol of Christ's blood-shedding. Such symbolism is devout and moving; but it is an innovation, and confuses the relationship between the emergent eucharistic shape and its origins in the Supper.

Unless you want to go back to the 'Seven-Action Shape' (which is rather pointless without the roast lamb and the herbs, and in any case falls between two stools in failing both to reproduce *all* the Supper and also to complete the transformation of the *Pesah* which Jesus himself began by abstaining), the emergent 'Shape of the Liturgy' as it provides a setting for the Thanksgiving Prayer is this:

1 (Taking +) Thanking;
2 Breaking.
3 Eating and Drinking.

Word and Response

Thanksgiving-as-obedience and Thanksgiving-as-remembrance belong clearly within a pattern of divine initiative and human response, the *Wort-Anwort* schema that has been the foundation of recent biblical theology. The liturgical shape which in East and West expresses this principle (Mass of the Catechumens–Mass of the Faithful, Preaching Service–Lord's Supper) is a wonderful catechetical tool for bringing home the principle itself – 'we love, because he first loved us'. It is, however, not sacrosanct; not, at least on historical grounds, for it is not certain that the pattern found in Justin was universally observed in the New Testament Church. Paul does indeed give a picture of the Christian assembly beginning in a ragged way, with some coming early and some late enough for the first lot to have a square meal before the other lot appear, and yet all of them arriving primed to contribute something, 'a hymn, a word of instruction, a revelation, a tongue or an interpretation' (1 Cor. 14.26, cf. Eph. 5.19–20; and set this with 1 Cor. 11.17–34); and it suggests a mingling of meal and devout entertainment that was not unknown in the Greek world. Its very Hellenistic character could give rise to serious understandings,[11] and the move to a settled and predictable structure, with teaching distinct from the meal, was a prudent one. It has been urged that Jewish models from the synagogue determined the Word-service, but the Passover pattern, with the Commemoration of Exodus before the meal, is a stranger candidate for this office than anything from the synagogue.

The question is of more than historical interest. In the present rediscovery of small-group worship, to say nothing of the charismatic movement, the various possibilities of combining Bible-fellowship with table-fellowship deserve exploring.

As far back as we can trace, the Word–Sacrament pattern has allowed for the aesthetic (and intellectual) need for *crescendo* and *decrescendo*. The rite as an entity has two peaks, the Gospel reading or the sermon, and Thanksgiving + Communion, with a lengthy *crescendo* before the former, a short swoop between the two, and an abrupt *decrescendo* after the second. The concluding *decrescendo* has never been adequate, as is evidenced by such devices as the 'Last Gospel'.

Different trajectories through the essential elements of the Word + Sacrament rite are also possible, especially if certain secondary elements may be moved.

Where, for example, should the Confession be? Among the 'prayers at the foot of the altar', *alias* 'The Preparation'? After all, many people are not at ease in approaching God before they have confessed. A case can still be made for deferring it until after the reading and exposition of the Word, for Christian repentance is more than spontaneous remorse, and needs to be informed by the Gospel; and yet providing different slots in one standard order of service is not a helpful way to combine both insights. Another method might be to place confession early in the rite for most Sundays, and to have a wholly different order for seasons of renewal, with the preaching leading into full confession and absolution, with perhaps the affirmation of vows. The 1975 Methodist Covenant Service, which weakened Robson's corporate self-examination and confession, and squeezed the neurasthenic remains into the Roman position for the sake of uniformity with the 'Sunday Service', was more than a missed opportunity, it was a disaster.

What, also, of the Peace (if it must be in church and not in the porch)? There is much to be said for this too to follow the Word, for fellowship needs renewing and correcting in the light of the Word, whether it precedes the intercessions[12], the creed, the offertory, or the communion. There may be grounds here too for seasonal variation; and why might it not sometimes be given at the very opening, as some early Roman *Ordines* seem to imply?

Then what of the Offering? (We leave aside the related but distinct matter of eucharistic oblation.) This is not specifically a eucharistic issue, but one touching the whole economy of incarnation. Since our flesh and its relation with the Father are remade through Christ, we have the liberty of offering ourselves, and all the creation entrusted to us, to God. For those baptized at their choice, this takes place before their baptism, in the profession of repentance and faith before the pouring[13] of the water. In the Eucharist, the natural setting for such offering is in response to the Word, and at the setting of the Table, on the model of King David's 'Thine own of thine own do we give thee' (1 Chron. 29.14), offering in worship gifts destined for *future* use in worship, for *future* consecration. The fullness of *self*-oblation belongs in the Thanksgiving–Communion complex, because of the unique intimacy between Christ and the members of his Body. The Laying of the Table should be an offering of *things*.

Lastly: the Intercessions. The force of tradition, that has led all liturgical reformers to place the intercessions after the sermon and before the laying of the table, is very strong; but pastoral considerations do not wholly support it. It is dubiously satisfactory to encourage a congregation to make post-communion euphoria the climax of the rite; moreover, activist dismissals and self-oblations carefully put into the non-Pelagian autoclave of the post-communion slot do not, unaccountably, rescue the situation. In John's interpretation of the Supper, the Lord's own intercession is the closing act (John 17), while they are all on their feet (John 14.31). Just so did *Birkat ha-Mazon* (and *Didache* 10) make intercession a climactic element in the Jewish and Christian Passover. What better use of our reaffirmed and revitalized oneness with Christ than to enter into his endless compassion for the world in which we are about to resume our daily place and work? Yet the pattern exemplified by Jesus himself has been hardly followed in the Church. Is there any excuse?

Intended Shape, Inherent Shape and Perceived Shape

Leaders of worship cannot evade the responsibility for enabling their fellow-worshippers to move together through worship as through a significant and rational progress of adoration. There will come times when all that is required is a leading of the service, without explanation, simply from accustomed act to accustomed act, without haste, yet not so slow as to lose the momentum. Other times will call for invitation, simplification, comment, patient introduction into the sequence of the People's Work for a People still fragmented, anxious, searching. There will never be a time this side of the Judgement when leaders of worship can afford to get so lost in personal rapture that they can ignore the people's needs of each day.

In a church with settled liturgies, the role of the pastor as mystagogue requires at least a minimal study of the intended shape written into the rites by the liturgy-makers. In a church that asks its ministers to be each one his or her own Liturgical Commission, the task is only superficially different: the common vocation of them all is to seek order for worship and the rest of life from the priorities of the gospel, and to share it.

Leaders of worship and makers of liturgies are only helpers; they do not determine the eventual unfolding of the worship-event. The shape they have designed, the shape they have expounded, may not be clear to others, and may be supplanted in use by other sequences which may none the less be inherent in their work though they did not see it. But that is not their concern. Their business is to offer the Church of their best, and to live with the results.

The factors which determine the shape of liturgy as it is lived are three:

First is the logicality of Christ the Logos, who can bring order to be through all forms of chaos, collective and subjective.

The second is the vitality of Christ, in whose Body tradition is life and growth, not inertia; within that life, every liturgical arrangement is provisional

The third is the endless adaptability of Christ, who, when lifted up from the earth, has power to bring all human beings to himself.

Perception of shape in worship by individuals and congregations is endlessly varied, and at the (to us) unpredictable mercy of time, place, mood, culture, prejudice, vice and virtue. To lead worship, to interpret it, is to act in the faith that

> God is his own interpreter,
> And he will make it plain,

that he will lead diverse, perverse, even irreconcilable perceptions into the adoring knowledge of himself.

Ransom, the hero of C. S. Lewis's *Voyage to Venus* (Ch. 17),

thought he saw the Great Dance. It seemed to be woven out of the intertwining undulation of many cords or bands of light, leaping over and under one another and mutually embraced in arabesques and flower-like subtleties. Each figure as he looked at it became the master-figure or focus of the whole spectacle, by means of which his eye disentangled all else and brought it into unity – to be itself entangled when he looked to what he had taken for mere marginal decorations and found that there also the same hegemony was claimed, and the claim made good, yet the former pattern not thereby dispossessed but finding in its new subordination a significance greater than that which it had abdicated.

No less may worshippers perceive the harmony of movements in the Great Dance of praise – but not as spectators, as dancers.

CONCLUDING NOTE: Lastly, back to Hoyle's cloud; its urgent voyage is to visit the site of the total dissolution of one of its fellow-clouds. This dissolution takes place only when a cloud has penetrated the secret of the purpose of the universe. When this happens, the energy released is so massive that all the other clouds feel it, and gather there with the utmost speed in hope of learning the secret for themselves. For them, the knowledge of the Absolute is the dominant aim of their existence. They pursue this mystical knowledge and are ready to pay everything to enter into it. *Verb. sap.?*

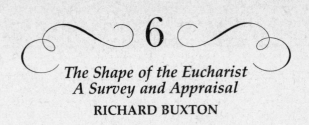

6

The Shape of the Eucharist
A Survey and Appraisal

RICHARD BUXTON

It is now nearly forty years since Gregory Dix fundamentally changed our appreciation of the eucharistic pattern by directing the search for eucharistic origins away from attempts to reconstruct the one original eucharistic prayer towards the idea that there was a primitive and universal shape, and that the histories of the major eucharistic liturgies should be seen as developments from this. The concept of shape in the Eucharist has been one of the dominant themes of liturgical scholarship since his book was published, and it has been a seminal influence on the revised and new rites of all the major Western churches, which have produced them in such abundance during the last twenty-five years. The middle of the twentieth century will go down in history as one of the great periods of Western liturgical creativity.

This does seem therefore a good time at which to look briefly at the history of the, mainly Western, eucharistic liturgy from the point of view of the concept of shape, in order to try to see how well it has served us.

Any comprehensive look at liturgical shape must start with the Last Supper. Between this and the emergence of the classical liturgies of the fourth century, certain landmarks are few and far between, and in consequence great care has to be taken with the interpretation of such evidence as does exist.

What can be said about the shape of the Last Supper? First of all that it was a full meal, and not simply a token eating and drinking. Second, the setting was intimate and domestic, a celebration by a small group of people who knew each other very well. Third, whether or not it was the actual Passover meal, it was anticipated as the celebration of Passover by Jesus and his disciples: the way the New Testament and subsequent tradition interprets it makes no sense otherwise. Fourth, Jesus converts it from the anamnesis of the Passover into the anamnesis of himself. The word anamnesis is used because no one English word expresses its meaning of calling into present reality a fresh liberation of the salvific power of the event remembered. Fifth, Jesus does this by what he does with bread and wine, which hereafter are the substance of the Christian Eucharist.

The way the growing Christian communities celebrated this over the first two centuries is very difficult to discern since our evidence is so elusive and fragmentary, so one is confined to making a few general statements that do seem secure. First of these is that the framework of the meal was lost very early on,[1] leaving the preparation of food, and the eating and the drinking token and symbolic, satisfying the soul, but leaving the physical needs of the body to be catered for elsewhere. Second, and surely a consequence of the first, the consolidation of the thanksgivings (or blessings) over the bread and wine into a unity, the eucharistic prayer, with a 'bread–wine' order of reference and of communion, rapidly becoming the normal and eventual universal order. Third, the preceding of the eucharistic action with other important things that the Christian community needed to do when it met for worship, normally a ministry of the word, but on special occasions other events such as a baptism or an ordination. Of course the whole of the Passover meal had been didactic within itself: but with the eucharistic action shrinking into a short symbolic activity, the didactic element needed resupplying from elsewhere, hence the prefixing of the ministry of the word. Fourth, the setting was still intimate, small scale and domestic and 'gathered round the table' in style. Fifth, and in contrast to the Passover, it was not the celebration of the human family conducted by the head of the household, but of the Church, the Body of Christ, presided over by the leaders of the Christian community, the bishop and clergy.[2]

One of the few firm landmarks in this period is Justin's account of the Eucharist, and he writes as follows of the normal Sunday liturgy (*c* 150 AD):

And on the day called Sunday an assembly is held in one place of all who live in town or country, and the records of the apostles or writings of the prophets are read for as long as time allows. Then, when the reader has finished, the president in a discourse admonishes and exhorts [us] to imitate these good things. Then we all stand up together and offer prayers; ... when we have finished praying, bread and wine and water are brought up, and the president offers prayers and thanksgivings to the best of his ability, and the people assent, saying the Amen; and there is a distribution, and everyone participates in [the elements] over which thanks have been given . . .[3]

This is quite recognizable as being the same in basic outline as any modern Western communion service,[4] with its order of readings, sermon, intercession, and eucharistic action. The latter Dix described as the classical four-action shape, but it is probably better to see it as two major actions, namely thanksgiving and reception, accompanied by two minor ones that are there for purely utilitarian reasons, whatever symbolic reasons became attached to them later on, for the elements have to be prepared on the table before thanks can be given over them, and a piece of bread has to be broken before it can be shared among a number of people (Justin does not mention a fraction or breaking).

In the fourth century the Church emerged from the relative obscurity imposed on it by the ever-present threat of persecution into a fully public life, recognized and approved of by the society in which it was now living. For several centuries after this the basic shape of the liturgy was scarcely altered; what did change was the style in which the basic shape was celebrated.

The way this changed was the almost inevitable consequence of moving the liturgy from its pre-Nicene domestic setting into the basilica, from the drawing-room into the public meeting hall. The liturgy becomes much more ceremonious. Instead of all gathering informally, the leaders of the worship now enter in solemn procession. Instead of a simple laying of the table, a formalized ritual develops for this, the seed that was to give rise in time to the luxurious growth of medieval offertory ceremonies.

The liturgy becomes hierarchical in character, with the clergy becoming much more sharply distinguished from the rest of the worshippers. Not that there is yet any essential change in function between the various orders of clergy and laity in eucharistic worship from what had prevailed before the peace of the Church under Constantine. Simply what had been obvious and implicit in the small-scale domesticity of early Christian worship was now made explicit by ceremony, movement and special vesture.

Next the liturgy began to acquire additional elements, notably musical items with a heavy emphasis on psalmody, partly for its own sake but also to cover other items that now took an appreciable amount of time. Examples of these are the chants between the various lessons, put in to fill the time it took to get the right persons and the right books to the right places that they might be read, and the laying of the table.

These were all developments made inevitable and necessary by the change in scale in which the Eucharist was celebrated. But in respect of the most important fundamentals the liturgy did not change between Justin and the description of the seventh/ eighth century Roman rite found in *Ordo Romanus Primus*.[5] In spite of the elaboration that has taken place the basic shape found in Justin is still clearly recognizable in *Ordo I*; moreover the rite is still corporate and vernacular, and all present share in the fullness of the rite itself, including reception of communion. Most important of all perhaps is that it is still 'gathered round the table' in style.

However the domesticity of the early celebration had been finally lost, and remained lost until its recovery in the modern house-church movement, and even here the long shadows of our ecclesiastical past often continue to hang over what is done.[6] Low mass (a medieval invention) and an early morning said Anglican celebration (a Victorian invention) may sometimes be small scale and intimate – they are certainly not domestic.

The changes that occurred in the late medieval period broke up this patristic unity of shape, and what happened prevented worshippers from having even an unconscious appreciation of it. It is to be doubted that many people earlier had a conscious appreciation of the shape, but it was there and it would have imprinted itself into the minds of the participants. What was serious about the medieval development was that after it had taken place it was no longer possible to have even an unconscious sense of shape, for one of the great anchors to the classical period of liturgical development had been knocked away.

Of the changes that occurred in the later medieval period, some were much more important from the point of view of shape than others. Certainly those additions that Dix referred to as the third stratum[7] do not seem to have been very important in this respect; they did not obscure the shape but overlay one that was already obscured.

Factors that are important were the loss of verbal understanding, doctrinal changes that focused far too much attention on particular moments in the rite, and on unprimitive innovations at that, and excessive concentration on the liturgy of the celebrant (and possibly other sacred ministers) with the consequent reduction of the role of the laity to that of being passive spectators, whose minds were often occupied with devotions quite unconnected with the liturgy and its shape as such.

Most crucial of all perhaps was the change from the 'gathered round the table' style to one involving the whole body of worshippers, clergy and laity, being in serried ranks facing in the same direction towards the altar or some imaginary focus of devotion on or beyond it. Perhaps a suitable metaphor for this style would be that of an army on parade with its officers at its head. This change is usually described as being from westward-facing celebration to eastward, but this is surely to place far too much emphasis on the position and attitude of the officiating minister; that people should think in this way at all is an unconscious echo of the excessive clericalization of the liturgy that developed in the late medieval period. What is really important about this is the changes in attitude of the whole body of worshippers, and the relationships that its various members have with one another.[8]

The Reformation crisis provoked a series of liturgical revolutions in countries that became Protestant. The composers of the reformed rites were above all concerned that the words of their liturgies should teach what they regarded as correct doctrine about the Lord's Supper, and should thus provoke the proper spiritual response from the worshipper. The result is often services that seem verbose in the extreme and in terms of overall form appear characterized by shapelessness rather than anything else.

Nevertheless it is possible to see in some reformed rites quite definite shapes, and sometimes ones that are wholly different from the classical shape of the patristic liturgy. For example a quite characteristic shape can be seen in the English 1552 rite, namely a threefold movement upwards from penance to a climax of praise, that is from the Collect for Purity to the Creed, exhortations to Sanctus and Prayer of Humble Access to Gloria.[9] Cranmer was a brilliant liturgical composer and quite able to see, as most writers of Reformation liturgies appear not to have done, that a liturgy must have form and shape as well as content, and that to be effective and usable the two must reinforce one another. But the 1552 service has very seldom been seen like this, for most people who have used its slightly but increasingly modified successors from 1559 onwards have not been Cranmerian in their eucharistic theology and those that have have been those who on the whole have been least interested in liturgy as such, let alone its shape.[10]

On the other hand the communion rite of the Scottish Book of Common Prayer of 1637 did restore something very similar to the classical eucharistic shape (apart from the misplaced laying of the table at the beginning of the intercession). This rite deserves far more attention than it has ever received in England, for it stands as the finest liturgical expression of the genius of classical seventeenth-century Anglicanism. Anglicanism should, incidentally, be regarded as a seventeenth-century religious tradition, not as a sixteenth-century one, for the latter merely laid the foundations and provided the raw materials on which the later century was to build. The Scots and the Americans have had the good sense to continue to build their eucharistic tradition on the basis of 1637, and it is perhaps no accident that a new American Prayer Book bids fair to be regarded as the best of all the very recent new Anglican Prayer Books. But in England the adoption of a 1637 style of liturgy was a political impossibility; had it not been so it is plausible to conjecture that the subsequent liturgical history of the Church of England would have been much less fraught with tension, controversy and bitterness than it in fact was. Had 1637 been the English communion service, the Tractarians would have had a eucharistic liturgy of the right shape upon which to build, instead of one whose incompatibility with what they came to believe about the Eucharist became increasingly apparent as time progressed. This incompatibility is demonstrated by the way their successors altered, modified and changed the 1662 rite, however much they attempted to expound it as enshrining their own views of the Eucharist, albeit sometimes arguing that it does this in embryonic form only. This process has had a number of very unfortunate consequences for the Church of England, both the destruction beyond any possibility of recall of the ideal of 'common prayer', and the fact that almost no one properly understands what the eucharistic doctrine of the 1662 Book of Common Prayer really is.

Since the 1637 rite expresses the ideals of classical Anglicanism much better than that of 1662, its adoption by the English Church in the seventeenth century, or that of something very like it, might have prevented much of the above happening and have kept many 'high church' Anglicans much closer to the genuine Anglican tradition than they have in fact stayed. Thus we might have been spared the very curious spectacle of certain sections of Anglicanism becoming ritual fossils of liturgical attitudes and practices discarded in the Roman Catholic Church since Vatican II. Whether a 1637 style liturgy would have created difficulties for the few genuine successors of Cranmer to the point of virtual exclusion from the Church of England is another matter.

However, all this is something of a digression, and rites produced between the middle of the sixteenth century and the early twentieth century that show clear signs of being influenced by considerations of shape in their composition are the exception rather than the rule. This stricture applies also to the Tridentine revision of the liturgy in the Roman Catholic Church, whose basic effect was to fasten a scarcely reformed medievalism on that Church for nearly another four centuries.

Several instances of this can be cited. First the people continued to be excluded from effective participation in the liturgy, firstly because of the ideology of the priesthood that had grown up in the medieval period, which the Counter-Reformation and suceeding centuries immensely strengthened by attempting to give it theological justification. And second, because mass continued to be said in Latin, which as the years passed became further from the vernacular than ever for most people. This means that the people's worship had to be stimulated by what could accompany that worship, for example a variety of devotional exercises, or the musical setting – and the Latin liturgy has been the stimulus for the composition of much very great music over the years.

Of course the visible and ceremonial accompaniments remained, but even here the greatest prominence continued to be given to precisely those things that were innovations in the late medieval period, for example the elevations during the institution narrative in the canon, which in themselves were witnesses to the thoroughly unprimitive and unfortunate changes in doctrinal understanding that took place at that time. Likewise medieval ideas about sacrifice in the Eucharist, and the medieval elaboration of offertory prayers that went with them, were retained.

Now it is not being claimed that the Tridentine reforms achieved nothing; clearly they did, in that much of the worst of the medieval clutter was swept away. Likewise the Counter-Reformation bore much fruit in genuine and deep spiritual devotion and heroic examples of Christian discipleship. What however is true is that the political and ecclesiastical situation produced by the crisis of the Reformation, and the primitive state of liturgical knowledge available at the time, prevented the sixteenth-century Roman Church achieving any deep-rooted reform of the methods of celebration and doctrine that had become associated with the Latin rite in the late medieval period. Indeed Counter-Reformation polemic provided reinforcement for precisely these things. The centuries of participative liturgical continuity from Justin to the *Ordo Romanus Primus* remained as obscured from sight as ever. Only with the liturgical movement in this century did things begin to change, and this paved the way for the liturgical revolution started by the Second Vatican Council.[11]

Many factors have made the twentieth century an era of great liturgical change for most of the Western churches, among them dissatisfaction with inherited liturgical traditions and the realization that they could no longer serve the needs of the worshipping Church in the present age, and the tremendous advances in liturgical scholarship that have been made during the last hundred years. This scholarship has affected every part of liturgy and every aspect of eucharistic worship, so prayers have been rewritten and new ones composed, the component parts of the service rearranged, ceremonial changed, the architectural setting frequently reordered, and new lectionaries drawn up. In the earlier part of the century each church involved in this process tended to do it in its own way, but as time has gone on liturgical scholarship has become increasingly ecumenical, and so have its fruits in the revised rites of the Western churches.

In all this activity shape seems to be the common unifying factor above all others, as a glance at the Roman Catholic missal of 1969, the Church of England Alternative Service Book of 1980,[12] the Methodist Service Book of 1975, and the United Reformed Church Book of Services 1980 will demonstrate, to name but a few important and mainly English examples. And the shape that has been followed is that enunciated by Dix nearly forty years ago.[13] Of course characteristics from the previous traditions of the churches concerned remain, for example the separate reading of the institution narrative as a warrant for the celebration prior to the Thanksgiving in the URC rite, and the greater elaboration of offertory prayers in the Roman rite. Likewise it is also obvious that a fair amount of detailed cross-borrowing has taken place between some of them. But the fundamental concept that unites them all is their shape, that of ministry of the word followed by ministry of the Eucharist, with the latter clearly following the outline put forward by Dix, even if it has been modified in detail as it has needed to be.

Shape, then, is one of the dominant concepts of modern eucharistic liturgy. Is it a good principle to build upon?

Shape as the fundamental guiding concept for modern liturgical construction had had extremely beneficial ecumenical consequences because scholars and liturgical commissions[14] are agreed about it across the boundaries of the major Western denominations. In terms of shape there has been a real convergence in modern eucharistic worship in a way that would have been undreamed of a couple of generations ago.

But having made shape one of the dominant considerations in the way our liturgies have been reordered, those who worship by modern rites need to take this into account in the way they use them. A number of points can be made under this general heading.

First the underlying shape of the liturgy must be apparent in the way it is performed, so that awareness of it can sink into the unconscious minds of the worshippers and the rite will develop a natural flow of its own. In this way people will be free to concentrate on the words and actions of the service, in particular the variable sections. Many modern liturgies are very permissive in the way they are ordered, with many optional items. The temptation to use all of them every time because the members of a congregation between them are attached to everything in the rite must be resisted, for this results in the celebration becoming a jumbled rush through the whole mass of material that obscures its shape, and prevents proper attention being paid to anything. The optional elements should be carefully weighed to see that they really are needed at that particular celebration, and full opportunity taken to vary them with time in the continuing life of a congregation. If, underlying this, the shape is constant and apparent, confusion will not result and the stranger in the midst will have no difficulty relating to what is going on.

Likewise the shape should not be obscured by the continuing use of ceremonies that arose to give expression to a different understanding of liturgical theology. A prime example of this is the elevation of the elements during the recital of the institution narrative, sometimes accompanied by the ringing of a gong or bells and censing. If it is desired to perpetuate these ceremonies at all – and as a visible and non-verbal assent to what is going on they can serve a good purpose – they should be done at the end of the Thanksgiving where they do not disturb its unity but enhance the climax of praise with which it concludes. Modern 'Catholic' liturgy should not make the early Protestant mistake of imposing an over-cerebral puritanism on its worship.

Another important point is that the method of celebration should not do violence to the architectural setting in which it is performed. It is quite right that a 'gathered round the table' style has once again become the predominant mode of celebration, but there are many churches that simply cannot be adapted to this, and if they cannot it should not be attempted. Eastward facing can be just as effective, particularly in a small church and, where everything else has been got right, it has insights of its own to contribute. Likewise, what is done in a house celebration should be truly domestic in scale and character.

Another important point is that the concept of shape permits the easy insertion of alternative prayers and other verbal forms, and the deletion of existing ones, when this is desired; if the shape remains constant, then the words can be altered within the continuity of a stable framework. In this way one of the pitfalls of a printed prayer book, even one as full of alternatives as the ASB, namely that it 'freezes' the liturgy, can be avoided, and the need for growth and development fostered. Similarly changes in doctrinal perception can be accommodated. One of the next great tasks of liturgical scholarship will be to look very seriously at the consequences for it of advances in biblical scholarship, changes in theological understanding, and properly absorbing the lessons of Church history, to say nothing of modern knowledge of the nature of the universe which is whole orders of magnitude different from and better than that which those who worked out the classical formularies of the Christian faith possessed. This task will be made immeasurably easier by the existence of an agreed and clear shape for the liturgy.

Above all full advantage should be taken of the flexibility and freedom of modern rites, combined with a good appreciation of their underlying unity of shape. Given this, the shape of the liturgy has proved to be a remarkably valuable cornerstone in liturgical reconstruction, and should continue to do so in use.

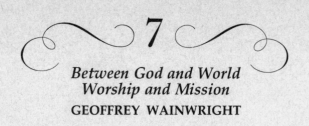

7

Between God and World
Worship and Mission

GEOFFREY WAINWRIGHT

Christian liturgy, and the Eucharist in particular, epitomizes not only the relations between the Church and God but also the relations between the Church and the world. It would be a mistake simply to designate these two sets of relations the vertical and the horizontal respectively. That would risk obscuring any direct contact between God and the world. Nevertheless the Church does occupy a mediating place and function between God and the world, between the world and God. The Church has the missionary task of proclaiming God's gospel to the world. In the other direction, the Church's responsibility is to represent the world before God in worship. The Church's mission in the world is not only evangelistic but also liturgical. The Church's worship of God finds not only liturgical but also evangelistic expression. Nor may liturgy and evangelism be separated from ethics: everyday behaviour takes place before God, and the conduct of Christians is part of their witness to the world; the liturgy gathers the ethical and evangelistic offering to a symbolic focus, from which point the love of God may irradiate the world the more brightly for having once again expressed itself in its own appointed way. In words from John and Charles Wesley's *Hymns on the Lord's Supper:*

> Jesu, we thus obey
> Thy last and kindest word,
> Here in thine own appointed way
> We come to meet Thee, Lord.

My intention in this essay is to indicate some of the perennial questions involved in the Church's existence at the hinge between God and world.[1] In some cases, I will sharpen the

94

issues to their acute contemporary form. The headings of the discussion are five prominent New Testament themes, which will be typified by some Pauline or near-Pauline texts. The titles are: 1. Reconciliation; 2. Evangelism; 3. Ethics; 4. Intercession; 5. Kingdom.

1 Reconciliation

(a) *Through Christ we both have access in one Spirit to the Father*
     (Ephesians 2.18)

In the second half of Chapter 2, the writer of the Letter to the Ephesians grounds the newly-created peace between Jew and Gentile in the reconciliation which the cross of Jesus Christ has effected for Jew and Gentile alike with God (v. 16). When Christ himself is said to be 'our peace' (v. 14), a 'peace-offering' may perhaps be understood, as the reference to Christ's blood in verse 13 suggests. The scope of the reconciliation is truly universal: making peace by the blood of Christ's cross, God was pleased to reconcile to himself all things, whether on earth or in heaven (Col. 1.20). The blood by which we are justified, the death by which we are reconciled to God, are those of God's Son; the initiative and work of reconciliation are therefore God's: 'God shows his love for us in that while we were yet sinners Christ died for us' (Rom. 5.6–11). That is why the liturgy which derives from the completed work of Christ is first and foremost the 'presence and act of the trinitarian God'.[2] As the Greek Orthodox theologian Nikos Nissiotis continues: 'Worship is not primarily man's initiative but God's redeeming act in Christ through his Spirit. The eucharistic sacrifice as the centre of Christian worship implies the absolute priority of God and his act before man's "answer" and "acknowledgment", as we usually describe Christian worship.'

But then Christian worship *is* our response, for through Christ we do have access in the Spirit to the Father (Eph. 2.18). Christ offered himself, through the eternal Spirit, without blemish to God (Heb. 9.14); and because we thus have a great high priest who has passed through the heavens, we may now with confidence draw near to the throne of grace (4.14–16) and are thereby enabled to serve the living God (9.14 again; cf. 10.19–25). *Proserchesthai*, to draw near, and *latreuein*, to serve, are cultic terms. In his treatise *On Prayer*, Origen argued – in his own origenistic way – that prayer is properly addressed to God through Christ in the Spirit. As Basil the Great was to show a century later against the Arians in his work *On the Holy Spirit*, this is the proper pattern for thanksgiving even according to developed trinitarian theology. It has remained the classical form of the mass, where we celebrate and enjoy our reconciliation to God.

(b) *So we are ambassadors for Christ, God making his appeal through us. We beseech you on behalf of Christ, be reconciled to God (2 Corinthians 5.20)*

God was in Christ reconciling *the world* to himself (2 Cor. 5.19). Those who, with the apostle, have let themselves be reconciled to God through Christ have thereby themselves been given 'a ministry of reconciliation' (v. 18). The embassy is addressed to all humanity: let yourselves be reconciled to God (v. 20). The ambassadorial style is that of plea and persuasion: 'the request is the evangelical form of authority'.[3] It is of the nature of reconciliation that it only takes place when the offer is received. The manner of the Church's message must respect the dignity of those from whom, through its medium, God is seeking a free response. Only so will the Church's preaching be *hyper Christou*, the phrase used twice in 2 Corinthians 5.20. The preached 'word of Christ' (Rom. 10.17) must correspond to the Word made flesh, who in christological self-surrender offered himself to men for acceptance or rejection. The best sacramental match to the news of the gospel is baptism upon profession of faith in the God who, by the Holy Spirit (1 Cor. 12.13), enables people to recognize the lordship of Jesus Christ who in cross and resurrection embodied the saving reconciliation of sinners to the Father, so that 'they might live no longer for themselves but for him who for their sake died and was raised' (2 Cor. 5.15). As St Paul puts it in a baptismally flavoured passage: 'If you confess with your lips that Jesus is Lord and believe in your heart that God raised him from the dead, you will be saved' (Rom. 10.9).

(c) *May God grant you to live in such harmony with one another, in accord with Christ Jesus, that together you may with one voice glorify the God and Father of our Lord Jesus Christ (Romans 15.5f)*

Since the reconciling God is 'a God of peace' (1 Cor. 14.33), those who let themselves be reconciled to him are expected to live harmoniously together (Rom. 12.16). Only so will they be able to worship God fittingly, that is, glorify him with one heart and one voice, *homothumadon en heni stomati* (Rom. 15.6). This applies not only when the assembly takes a charismatic turn, as in the situation which Paul is trying to regulate in 1 Corinthians 14. Divisive behaviour also nullifies the Lord's Supper as such, it is Paul's teaching in 1 Corinthians 11.17–34. That passage contains hints, especially in verses 21f and 33f, that the factions may have had a social and economic base, as is explicitly the case in the reproved discrimination between rich and poor in James 2.1–7. In contemporary Latin American Christianity, such is the tension between political oppressors and politically oppressed that 'participation in the Eucharist, as it is celebrated today, appears to many to be an action which, without an authentic Christian community underlying it, becomes an exercise in make-believe'.[4]

Gustavo Gutiérrez recognizes also the potential of the Eucharist for 'the building up of a real human brotherhood'. On the more private level, the modern liturgical movement's reintroduction of the exchange of peace among the congregation – already the Church of South India borrowed the practice from the Syrian communities – has proved to be a salutary encouragement to better personal relationships even in congregations composed of undemonstrative English people. The 'success' of the gesture is a tribute of intended obedience to the dominical injunction recorded in Matthew 5.23f: reconciliation within the Christian family was early expressed and preserved by the 'holy kiss' mentioned several times in the New Testament epistles, though the *pax* before sharing together in the Eucharist regrettably assumed a clericalized form in the classical Byzantine and Latin rites.

Denominationalism being theologically unjustifiable, indeed absurd (1 Cor. 1.10–17), the separated communities have the plain duty to press urgently on towards that 'visible unity in one faith and in one eucharistic fellowship' which the member churches of the World Council of Churches set themselves to achieve. As an English Methodist, I make once more an evangelical appeal to the Church of England to join wholeheartedly in the reconciliation which other churches in the country are seeking. Attempts at reconciliation are undergirded by the Lord's own prayer 'that they all may be one'. From the beginning, the modern ecumenical movement has seen Christian unity to be part and parcel of the Church's witness to the world: 'that the world may believe' (John 17.20–23). Disunity among Christians is active counter-testimony to the gospel of reconciliation.

(*d*) *If possible, so far as it depends on you, live peaceably with all*
(*Romans 12.18*)

That Christians should, as far as others allow, extend evangelical behaviour beyond the limits of the Church is a clear implication of the dominical teaching represented by Matthew 5.43–8 and already reflected in Romans 12.14–21. In their worship assembly, Christians have learnt and experienced peace, and all the other values of the divine kingdom, in an 'interior' and 'definitive' form; they should therefore, according to the analogical movement set forth by Karl Barth in his essay on *Church Community and Civil Community* (1946) seek the furtherance of these same values, at least in an 'exterior' and 'provisional' way, in the broader social realm. The particular importance of prayer for peace will be mentioned later.

Reconciliation is a key New Testament category for the statement of the gospel. The theme of this opening section has therefore been fundamental to all that now follows.

2 Evangelism

(*a*) *I am already on the point of being sacrificed; the time of my departure has come*
(*2 Timothy 4.6*)

The martyrdom which St Paul expected was but the culmination of an apostolate marked by 'afflictions, hardships, calamities, beatings, imprisonments, tumults, labours, watching, hunger' (2 Cor. 6.4f). He bore on his body the marks of Jesus (Gal. 6.17). In the trials of apostleship Paul believed that he was 'carrying in the body the death of Jesus': 'While we live we are always being given up to death for Jesus' sake, so that the life of Jesus may be manifested in our mortal flesh. So death is at work in us, but life in you' (2 Cor. 4.7–12). The cultic roots of this sacrificial language become unmistakable when the apostle writes: 'Even if I am to be poured out as a libation upon the sacrificial offering of your faith (*alla ei kai spendomai epi tēi thusiai kai leitourgiai tēs pisteōs humōn*), I am glad and rejoice with you all' (Phil. 2.17). The self-spending of the gospel-preacher is part of the larger offering that includes the converts' faith. The modern spread of Christianity in black Africa was dependent, under God, on the willingness of missionaries from our churches to enter 'the white man's grave': African Christians thankfully recognize that as a cause for rejoicing, whatever the ambiguities introduced by concomitant colonialism.

(b) *On some points I have written to you very boldly, by way of reminder, because of the grace given me by God to be a minister* [leitourgon] *of Christ Jesus to the Gentiles in the priestly service* [hierourgounta] *of the gospel of God, so that the offering* [prosphora] *of the Gentiles may be acceptable, sanctified by the Holy Spirit*
    (*Romans 15.15f*)

The offering of the Gentiles – it matters little whether the genitive is objective or subjective – is their 'obedience', which is 'the obedience of faith' (Rom. 1.5). As we have just seen under (*a*), the evangelist's evangelizing activity is itself worship of God: St Paul uses the verb *latreuein* in Romans 1.9, whose sense C. K. Barrett correctly captures with 'God, to whom I render spiritual service in proclaiming the gospel of his Son'.[5] When, in response to the preacher's message, conversions are made, the eucharistic chorus is thereby augmented: 'Since we have the same spirit of faith as he had who wrote, "I believed, and so I spoke," we too believe, and so we speak, knowing that he who raised the Lord Jesus will raise us also with Jesus and bring us with you into his presence. For it is all for your sake, so that as grace extends to more and more people, it may increase thanksgiving, to the glory of God' (2 Cor. 4.13–15).

In this connection, two questions may arise. First: is the liturgical assembly of the Christians itself directly evangelistic?

Second: how is the worship of others apart from Christians to be evaluated? These questions we address in turn.

(c) *But if all prophesy, and an unbeliever or outsider enters, he is convicted by all, he is called to account by all, the secrets of his heart are disclosed; and so, falling on his face, he will worship God and declare that God is really among you*
(*1 Corinthians 14.24f*)

The context in 1 Corinthians 14 makes clear that the prophetic message spoken in the Christian assembly is intended for believers. Believers need constantly to be confirmed in the gospel they have accepted. Yet when God's word is intelligibly spoken (the contrast is made with speaking in tongues), the apostle's expectation is that any entering unbelievers or outsiders will be persuaded to adoration (whereas from glossolalia they will infer madness). In so far as a *disciplina arcani* was observed in the early Church, its justification will have lain in the threat and actuality of persecution to which Christians were exposed. The deliberate closure of any occasion on which the gospel is proclaimed appears theologically contrary to the latter's character as an 'open secret'.[6]

But how far may the unconverted actively participate in what they witness? In 1 Corinthians 14.16, St Paul *may* be envisaging the possibility that an outsider will be led to say 'Amen' to *the* eucharistic prayer. The *Didache* used the dominical injunction not to cast pearls before swine in order to exclude the unbaptized from sharing in the agape or Eucharist. The Lord himself appears to have liberally fed all comers in the messianically significant desert-feedings. John Wesley considered the Lord's Supper a 'converting ordinance' and encouraged 'seekers' to communicate (admittedly he could presuppose an infant baptism, though the regeneration had been 'sinned away' and conversion was needed). My own view is that no one should be refused communion who has been moved by the celebration of the gospel sign then in progress to seek saving fellowship with the Lord through eating the sacramental bread and drinking the sacramental wine. Then such a person should be brought to the sealing commitment of baptism as expeditiously as possible.[7]

(d) *For, 'every one who calls upon the name of the Lord will be saved'*
(*Romans 10.13*)

The question may appear differently when it is a matter of 'dialogue with other religions' or of the 'religious' marking of 'civil' events in a religiously pluralist society. How far may non-Christians be invited to share in Christian worship? How far should Christians accept any invitations they may receive from adherents of other religions? Are 'joint services' permissible? In the contexts envisaged, the intention to 'convert' is generally reckoned to fall foul of the rules or spirit of the game. In some respects, the questions sound similar to those raised in the early days of the modern ecumenical movement among Christians; but a qualitative difference may be introduced by the issue of the uniquely saving name of the Lord Jesus Christ (cf. Acts 4.12).

The relations between Christ(ianity) and other religions will become an increasingly urgent question in the next generations, both in the 'one world' and in the particular context of Britain. It would probably be premature to attempt an answer already to what may be an old question but one which is now being posed in relatively new circumstances. John Hick desires a 'copernican revolution' in religious and theological understanding, whereby God would replace Christ at the centre, and Christianity join the other religions as the circling planets.[8] From a Christian viewpoint, it is hard to see how that could happen without such a forfeiture of devotional and doctrinal substance from our faith as to denature and devitalize it. It is more likely, and appropriate, that Christians will frame the debate in terms of an *exclusive* or a more *inclusive* understanding of the unique status and universal significance ascribed to Jesus Christ by the Christian confession of faith.

The inclusive alternative is as old as the view of Justin Martyr that the ancient Greeks who lived according to the Logos were Christians *avant la lettre*. It is expressed in a eucharistic prayer composed for the experimental *New Orders of the Mass for India* which have since been forbidden by Rome, apparently at the request of less 'inclusivist' Indian Catholics. The preface made successive allusions to the animistic religions, to Hinduism (with its three paths to salvation: *karma, jnana, bhakti*), to Buddhism and Jainism together, and finally to Islam:

> God of the nations,
> You are the desire and hope

of all who search for you with a sincere heart.
You are the Power almighty
adored as Presence hidden in nature.
You reveal yourself
to the seers in their quest for knowledge,
to devout who seek you through sacrifice and detachment,
to every man approaching you by the path of love.
You enlighten the hearts that long for release
by conquest of desire and universal kindness.
You show mercy to those who submit
to your inscrutable decrees.

The optional reading from Indian Scriptures was justified in terms of their containing 'seeds of the Word'. On the other hand, the second- and third-century Fathers, including Justin, looked upon the pagan mysteries as diabolical counterfeits of the Christian baptism and Eucharist. The exclusivist position, corresponding to 'Christ against culture' in H. R. Niebuhr's typology of attitudes, will doubtless continue to be maintained also, making reciprocal participation and common worship appear impossible between Christians and others.[9]

3 Ethics

(a) *I appeal to you therefore, brethren, by the mercies of God, to present your bodies as a living sacrifice* (thusian), *holy and acceptable to God, which is your spiritual worship* (logikēh latreian). *Do not be conformed to this world but be transformed by the renewal of your mind, that you may prove what is the will of God, what is good and acceptable and perfect*
(*Romans 12.1f*)

The ethical worship of God is made possible and necessary by the indwelling presence of the Holy Spirit. The cultic metaphor of the body as temple can be given an individual application: 'The immoral man sins against his body. Do you not know that your body is a temple of the Holy Spirit within you, which you have from God? You are not your own; you were bought with a price. So glorify God in your body' (1 Cor. 6.18–20). Or a rather more communal one: 'What agreement has the temple of God with idols? For we are the temple of the living God; as God said, "I will live in them and move among them, and I will be their God, and they shall be my people. Therefore come out from them, and be separate from them, says the Lord, and touch nothing unclean; then I will welcome you, and I will be a father to you, and you shall be my sons and daughters, says the Lord Almighty." Since we have these promises, beloved, let us cleanse ourselves from every defilement of body and spirit, and make holiness perfect in the fear of God' (2 Cor. 6.16—7.1).

The association, indeed identification, between sin and idolatry is made also in Colossians 3.5: 'Put to death therefore what is earthly in you: fornication, impurity, passion, evil desire, and covetousness, which is idolatry. On account of these the wrath of God is coming.' And again in Ephesians 5.5: 'Be sure of this, that no fornicator or impure man, or one who is covetous (that is, an idolater), has any inheritance in the kingdom of Christ and of God.' It is significant that baptismal imagery pervades the context of these verses: dying and rising with Christ (Col. 3.1–4), putting off the old and putting on the new (Col. 3.5,8,10,12,14; Eph. 4.22, 24, 25, 31), being renewed (Col. 3.10; Eph. 4.23), enlightened (Eph. 5.7–14), sealed (Eph. 4.30). Since Christians have passed through 'the washing of regeneration and renewal in the Holy Spirit' (Titus 3.5–7), the apostle has an indicative basis for the imperatives of Romans 12.1f: the renewed mind is to discern the will of God, and what is there found acceptable (*euareston*) is the criterion for bodily conduct which can be described as a sacrifice acceptable to God (*tōi theōi euareston*). The transformation of the believer means an end to conformity with this world. Ethics thereby become part of the Christian witness.

(b) *Maintain good conduct among the Gentiles, so that in case they speak against you as wrong-doers, they may see your good deeds and glorify God on the day of visitation*
(1 Peter 2.12)

The passages mentioned under (*a*) contrast the behaviour expected of Christians with the behaviour that characterized them before their conversion and still characterizes the pagan environment. The 'new creation' is ethically distinguishable from the old. When the First Letter of Peter evokes the eschatological prospect of 'the day of visitation', the thought may be partly of the *confusion* of non-believers as they are made to see the ultimate reversal of this-worldly values. But with 1 Corinthians 14.24f in mind, it may be possible to 'realize' the eschatology in such a way that non-believers are already conceived as being brought to repentance and faith and so to the positive glorification of God . . . by the witness of a distinctively Christian life. The judgemental aspect of Christian 'light' in respect of the world appears uppermost in Philippians 2.14–16: 'Do all things without grumbling or questioning, that you may be blameless and innocent, children of God without blemish in the midst of a crooked and perverse generation, among whom you shine as lights in the world, holding fast the word of life, so that in the day of Christ I may be proud that I did not run in vain or labour in vain.' The sentence used from Matthew 5.16 at the almsgiving in the communion office of the English Book of Common Prayer envisages positive doxology resulting: 'Let your light so shine before men, that they may see your good works, and glorify your Father which is in heaven.' By 'good works' which the world can understand, the Church witnesses to the *gracious end* into which the transitory world, if it will let itself be converted, is passing.[10]

4 Intercession

(a) *Continue steadfastly in prayer, being watchful in it with thanksgiving; and pray for us also, that God may open to us a door for the word, to declare the mystery of Christ, on account of which I am in prison, that I may make it clear, as I ought to speak* (*Colossians 4.2–4*)

St Paul's letters abound in the apostle's assurances to the recipients that he gives thanks to God for their having come to believe, and that he prays for the strengthening of their faith in whatever way circumstances require:[11] for example, Romans 1.8f; 1 Corinthians 1.4–9; Ephesians 1.15–23; 3.14–19; Philippians 1.3–11; Colossians 1.3–14; 1.29—2.7; 1 Thessalonians 1.2f; 2.13–16; 3.9f; 2 Thessalonians 1.3–12; 2.13–17; 2 Timothy 1.3–14. As we saw under 2(b) and 3 (b) in particular, the faith and works of the converts are themselves a continuation of the

Christian message before the world. In return, St Paul frequently asks the churches to pray for him in his apostolic labours: for example, Romans 15.30–32; 2 Corinthians 1.8–11; Ephesians 6.18–20; Philippians 1.12–26 (especially v. 19); Colossians 4.2–4; 1 Thessalonians 5.25; 2 Thessalonians 3.1–3.

Solidarity in mutual intercession is particulary valuable when engagement with a world which needs but resists the gospel brings Christians into distress. The famous Pauline 'collection' for the saints at Jerusalem makes concrete such solidarity and is a forerunner of modern programmes of inter-church aid.[12] An encouraging feature in the recent history of the World Council of Churches is the realization that material aid goes hand in hand with intercessory prayer: the Faith and Order Commission has produced an ecumenical prayer calendar which facilitates informed intercession for sister churches throughout the world.[13]

(b) *First of all, then, I urge that supplications, prayers, intercessions, and thanksgivings be made for all men, for kings and all who are in high positions, that we may lead a quiet and peaceable life, godly and respectable in every way. This is good, and it is acceptable in the sight of God our Saviour, who desires all men to be saved and to come to the knowledge of the truth. For there is one God, and there is one mediator between God and men, the man Christ Jesus, who gave himself as a ransom for all, the testimony to which was borne at the proper time. For this I was appointed a preacher and apostle . . . a teacher of the Gentiles in faith and truth*
(1 *Timothy* 2.1–7)

In the case of the secular authorities, the thanksgiving urged by the apostle will be on account of their God-given ministry to 'approve good conduct' and to 'execute God's wrath on the wrongdoer' (Rom. 13.1–7; cf. 1 Pet. 2.13f), to 'truly and indifferently minister justice, to the punishment of wickedness and vice, and to the maintenance of thy true religion, and virtue' (Book of Common Prayer). The thanksgiving for all people will be on account of God's universal saving intention (1 Tim. 2.3f): the 'general thanksgiving' of the Book of Common Prayer is a perfect example.

'Supplications, prayers and intercessions' for rulers have classically centred on their peace-keeping responsibilities:

besides being an analogous reflection of the *shalom* of the divine kingdom, peaceful conditions facilitate the travels and tasks of the evangelist. Prayers for 'all sorts and conditions of men' are most vitally prayers for the conversion of the world: such prayers figure prominently in the 'prayers of the faithful' in the ancient liturgies.[14] It is a patristic thought that Christian prayer contributes to the *preservation* of the world, so that all people may have time and opportunity to arrive at the faith before the final advent of Christ in judgement.[15] In all these ways, the Christian liturgy – performed through the one Mediator – appears truly as a *leitourgia*, a 'public service' to the world.

There is a groaning wherever Satan blocks the birth of the new creation, whether through unbelief, idolatry, individual sin, social injustice, physical suffering or mental torment. The same word 'groan' is used at Romans 8.22 for the sighing of creation (*sustenazei*), at 8.23 for the struggles of believers as they await full redemption (*stenazomen*), and at 8.26 for the Spirit-inspired prayers of Christians (*stenagmois alalētois*). Christians pray that the whole world may be set free to share in the glorious liberty that is the hope of the sons and daughters of God.[16]

5   Kingdom

The kingdom of God is not food and drink but righteousness and peace and joy in the Holy Spirit
(*Romans 14.17*)

The context of St Paul's remark is disputes over meat-eating and wine-drinking: the apostle rebukes those who, 'for the sake of food, destroy the work of God'. According to St Luke, the Lord will at the judgement reject the claim of the 'workers of iniquity' to have eaten and drunk in his presence (Luke 13.25–7). Yet the kingdom of God is pictured as a feast: 'And people will come from east and west, and from north and south, and sit at table in the kingdom of God' (Luke 13.29). It would capture the gist of biblical teaching concerning the messianic banquet if we were to paraphrase the apostle thus: The kingdom of God is food and drink *only in so far as* eating and drinking express justice, peace and joy in the Holy Spirit.

When any creature of God is received with thanksgiving (cf. 1 Tim. 4.3–5), its use becomes thereby an occasion and medium of communion with God. In what it does with the bread and wine over which it has given thanks, the eucharistic liturgy makes exemplary use of all food and drink as a medium of communion with God which cannot make abstraction of communion with fellow humans (cf. 1 John 4.7–21). Moreover, the general way in which people use all food and drink is itself a test of the way in which they are living before God and among themselves. Since the Eucharist is representative of all meals, and since all food and drink is representative of the totality of human life, the sacrament should be so ordered that it shows the kingdom of God to be food and drink *only upon condition that* their use embodies justice, peace, and joy in the Holy Ghost. A properly ordered Eucharist exemplifies justice because grateful people are all equally welcomed there by the merciful Lord into his table-fellowship and all together share in the fruits of redemption and in the foretaste of the new heavens and the new earth in which right will prevail (cf. 2 Pet. 3.13); it exemplifies peace, because reconciled people are there at peace with God and with one another; it exemplifies joy in the Holy Ghost, because the cup of blessing conveys to all who partake of it a taste of that 'sober intoxication' which the Spirit gives (cf. Eph. 5.18). Having learnt and experienced this in the paradigm of the eucharistic meal, the Church is committed to an everyday witness in word and deed which will give the opportunity for all the material resources of creation and all occasions of human contact to become the medium of that communion with God and among human beings which is marked by justice, peace, and joy in the Holy Ghost, and in which the kingdom of God consists.

A Eucharist understood and practised in that way will not fall victim to the Marxist critique of unconcern with this-worldly happiness. By its refusal, however, to abandon the strictly eschatological prospect, it will offer to satisfy the hunger which the sensitive among its marxist despisers feel for a transcendence and an ultimacy over which death will not triumph: the definitive and eternal kingdom of God.

Conclusion

By letting the liturgy appear as the ritual focus of the Church's evangelism and ethics, I hope to have pointed impatient

evangelists and ethicists to some values of the liturgy.[17] Granted
the insights of cultural anthropology concerning the place of
symbols in human existence, one could even speak of the
necessity of the liturgy in respect of evangelism and ethics. In the
other direction, I hope to have encouraged liturgists in their
belief that evangelism and ethics are their concern, too.

It will be fitting to conclude with the passage from the First
Letter of St Peter which integrates ethics and evangelism into a
liturgical edifice clearly shaped by baptism and Eucharist:

> You have been born anew, not of perishable seed but of
> imperishable, through the living and abiding word of God . . .
> That word is the good news which was preached to you. So
> put away all malice and all guile and insincerity and envy and
> all slander. Like newborn babes, long for the pure spiritual
> milk, that by it you may grow up to salvation; for you have
> tasted the kindness of the Lord. Come to him, to that living
> stone, rejected by men but in God's sight chosen and precious;
> and like living stones be yourselves built into a spiritual house,
> to be a holy priesthood, to offer spiritual sacrifices acceptable
> to God through Jesus Christ . . . You are a chosen race, a royal
> priesthood, a holy nation, God's own people, that you may
> declare the wonderful deeds of him who called you out of
> darkness into his marvellous light.

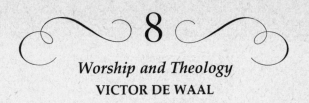

8

Worship and Theology
VICTOR DE WAAL

'Tell me the old, old story' – so begins a familiar Evangelical children's chorus. From the simplicity of a beach mission to the elaboration of a great liturgical ceremony every act of public worship has at its heart the telling of an old story. And the purpose of the service is to incorporate the participants in that story, to make them severally actors in its continuation. It is the sharing in common stories that makes any community what it distinctively is, children and neophytes must learn them, and the identity of the group is reaffirmed by their constant repetition. Pre-literate societies are known for the accuracy through many generations of the oral tradition of their myths, legends and folk-tales, and literacy gives rise to the careful preservation and rendering of texts. For the story and the community are bound up with each other, they have a common origin, and thus the authenticity of the story is as unquestioned as the existence of those who hear it, of whom it tells, and who continue to tell it themselves. To question the story is to doubt oneself, and a people that loses faith in its gods loses faith in itself, and vice versa.

How does such a community come to terms with change? For circumstances, the context of living, are bound to change, especially for a society with a long history, like a nation or a great religion. New events, new discoveries, new perspectives demand to be incorporated into the story, to be explained by it. We need to be sure that the story is still true, and in times of much external change the debate about the meaning of the story is charged with anxiety about the future of the community, for to change the story is to change the community.

That anxiety becomes all the more acute when the language in which the story is told is itself changed, for language is no aseptic tool. To separate the story and its language requires surgery of outstanding skill and delicacy if the story is to survive the operation, and the community with it, for while the meaning is neither in the story nor in the language alone, it is communicated in the union of the two, in resonances too subtle for quick dissection. As a community and the language it speaks are inseparable, so language and story belong to one another. And it is therefore not surprising that when the story-tellers change the language, they are suspected of designs on the story, and accused of destroying the society they are expected to uphold.

As story and community depend utterly for their existence one upon the other, it is immaterial which we think of as primary – the story did not exist before the community, neither did the community exist before the story. Mankind and history, Israel and the covenant, the Church and the gospel, each pair are coeval and co-terminous.

If the story is our starting point, we are presented at the outset with a text or texts – in the Christian case the Scriptures of the Old and New Testaments. But these texts, in so far as they are moulded by the languages and thought-forms of their authors and translators, contain already a degree of interpretation of the story, which in itself is inaccessible to us. The exegete will discover as accurately as he may the state of the best text and the meaning of its writers, but he cannot go behind and beyond them – to the purposes and action of God. It is only when, as it were, we ourselves enter the story, through our prayer, our worship and theology, that this access becomes possible. Here a second level of interpretation is inescapable, an interpretation crystallized in liturgies and creeds, in canons, moral codes, and orders of church life. And so we come to the visible societies of Christians who together make up that real, though intangible, entity – the Church living in the Holy Spirit.

Or, if we begin our analysis with the community, in our case the Church, then we can see how that Church is visible only through its members, who draw out of the depths of their common life the beliefs about faith and practice needful for that life; beliefs and practices explored in theology and expressed in forms of worship, which themselves originally found language to compose those texts that tell the story of man's intercourse with God, and then enshrined them in a canon.

Either way the pattern is the same. An origin and conclusion whose authenticity is by definition beyond question, revealed or infallible at most, inspired and indefectible at least, a revealed or inspired Bible, an infallible or indefectible Church; and a means whereby the truth is mediated to us, a locus of interpretation and accommodation to particular need and contemporary circumstance. The place and time *par excellence* of this mediation is the work of theology and the celebration of the liturgy. Through these the community is confronted again with its own story and enters into it, and the individual finds and claims his particular role and identity. Though we are speaking here of Christianity, the principle and pattern hold good for any community.

How then are worship and theology themselves related?

When asked to give an account of themselves, to explain what is distinctive of their Church, Anglicans have very generally appealed to the old motto *lex orandi, lex credendi* – the rule of prayer discloses the rule of faith. Thus on taking office every clergyman, from the Archbishop of Canterbury downwards, declares:

> I declare my belief in the faith which is revealed in the Holy Scriptures and set forth in the catholic creeds and to which the historic formularies of the Church of England bear witness; and in public prayer and administration of the sacraments, I will use only the forms of service which are authorized or allowed by Canon.

The historic formularies mentioned are, together with the Thirty-nine Articles, the Book of Common Prayer and the Ordering of Bishops, Priests and Deacons. And indeed, until recently, it was a matter of observation that Anglicans of very different churchmanship, and also the provinces of the Anglican Communion throughout the world, were united in their use, in some recognizable form, of the texts of the Prayer Book and of the Ordinal attached to it.

But now the process of liturgical revision throughout the Anglican Communion has meant that few of its member churches retain more than vestiges, as far as their texts are concerned, of that Prayer Book; and the Ordinal likewise has been universally revised. The daily services during the Lambeth Conference of 1978 at Canterbury when each church in turn celebrated the liturgy according to its own rite testified to this revolution. And the Church of England itself, in day-to-day use, has very generally and with extraordinary rapidity adopted the alternative services on their being authorized, the clergy and the theological colleges on the whole leading the way.

It is therefore not unreasonable to ask what the consequences of the relegation of the Book of Common Prayer and the Ordinal to the status of historic formularies will be both on Anglican doctrine and on the cohesiveness of the Anglican Communion. The Scriptures continue to be read, the creeds (though not that of 'St Athanasius') recited. No doubt the Prayer Book will in England continue to be used occasionally and studied as part of their training by the clergy, but it may be doubted whether it will occupy a much larger place in the life of the Church than the Thirty-nine Articles.

The alternative services in England, the new services in other Anglican churches, contain little that is distinctively Anglican, for they are the product of a liturgical scholarship that has from the outset transcended ecclesiastical divisions and frontiers, and has produced new liturgies of striking similarity in all denominations. Can Anglicanism as a particular theological tradition survive this cutting of its peculiar liturgical roots? Will the Anglican ethos be dissipated as a mist before the rising sun? Such hyperbole is not altogether out of place in the context of present controversy, in which a powerful faction is arguing, not merely that Anglicanism is under threat in the disuse of the Prayer Book, but that the very cultural soul of England and all that is distinctive of that culture is dying as a consequence. It is argued forcibly, and on the contrary, that it is high time that the Christian denominations overcome their differences, and that the liturgical movement in its production of common texts is proving a providential means to that end. Such an argument avails itself too of the motto *lex orandi, lex credendi*, and looks forward to the growth of theological unity on the basis of a confluence of forms of worship. And indeed it is remarkable, for example, how 'Anglican' much contemporary Roman Catholic worship in England now appears to an Anglican visitor – the Mass englished, the hymns very largely from Church of England

and Nonconformist sources, and the stripping of ornament consequential to a modern fashion for simplicity.

We may allow that there are grounds both for the fears of the one protagonist and for the hopes of the other, while not believing them to be necessarily mutually exclusive. For, on the one hand, whereas Anglicanism is indisputably rooted in its worship, this liturgical tradition is not only a matter of liturgical texts, but of how those texts are interpreted and used. On the other hand, the same consideration leads to the *caveat* that texts by themselves are unlikely greatly to change the ecumenical scene. Texts indeed provide the basis on which the self-understanding of a community depends, but only as the focus around which that self-understanding is worked out. To this process many other factors contribute and, as ecumenical discussions have repeatedly discovered, these factors are of comparable importance. The rule of prayer may disclose the rule of faith, but inversely, faith manifestly affects the forms of prayer.

While therefore it may be true that the distinctive theological perspective of Anglicanism has been in large measure nourished by the Prayer Book, it is equally true to say that the Prayer Book itself was produced by an Anglicanism which is perhaps capable of surviving it. Before the event it was surmised that the 1978 Lambeth Conference might well be the last of its kind, so little do the member churches now have outwardly in common, not even a common language. And yet, in the outcome, the bishops discovered among themselves a profound unity of approach which was particularly significant in those important matters in which differences of opinion were most sharp. It became again apparent that it is in its *theological method* that Anglicanism is distinctive, and which it can perhaps offer in contribution to other communions.

Here the history of the use of the Book of Common Prayer is itself instructive. Though it is the product of deliberate compromise, a compromise, it must be remembered, that even so failed to unite the whole spectrum of English religious life, those who did use it did so in widely varying ways. No play by Shakespeare has been more variously interpreted, produced and acted, not only in successive periods but by different companies during the same

113

period, than the Prayer Book service of Holy Communion.
During the hundred years from the mid-nineteenth to the mid-
twentieth centuries the contrast, let us say, between an
Evangelical evening celebration of the Holy Communion at
the north end of the table and an Anglo-Catholic non-
communicating High Mass (of course *never* in the evening) with
the Prayer Book texts intercalated with the Roman Missal could
hardly have been more startling. But for our purposes the
significance of this lies in the fact that the identical texts served
different, and indeed incompatible, theological interpretations.
And this was no new phenomenon to Anglicanism. The Johnson
case of 1570 is a case in point.[1] Johnson pleaded that in the
Communion service Cranmer had intended the words of
institution to stir the faith of the hearers, not in any way to
change the elements of bread and wine, and so, when wine
failed, he had not 'consecrated' again, but continued the
communion of the people with additional wine. His submission
as to Cranmer's intention was surely correct, but failed to
impress his judges who insisted on interpreting Cranmer's
liturgy according to an older tradition. Johnson found himself
beyond the limits of Anglican compromise, but the case
illustrates how a text can be stretched to bear a meaning not in
the intentions of its author. In the contrary sense Stephen
Gardiner had earlier, it will be remembered, sought to interpret
the 1549 rite from within his own medieval catholic tradition.

Such ambiguity is of course not peculiar to Anglicanism, as can
be seen from the problems medieval theologians had with the
Canon of the Roman Mass, once the theology of the liturgy had
become focused in the words of institution, and the
accompanying manual acts had begun to bear the substance of
the liturgical action. Offertory, Fraction and Communion itself
became secondary, and the commentators ask themselves
whether it is only tradition that argues the need for anything in
the Canon after the Consecration. One may speculate that the
English clergy's readiness to accept a 'Prayer of Consecration'
which concludes with the words of institution, and the
continental Protestants' dispensing with the Canon altogether,
was prepared for by just such commentary.

More curious still is that whole tradition of allegorical
commentary on the liturgy from Theodore of Mopsuestia

onwards which found increasingly fertile ground in Christian devotion as the texts themselves began to acquire the inviolability of sacred antiquity. The retention of Latin in the West, less and less generally understood, contributed to a significant shift in the balance of the liturgy. Hitherto the reading of the Scriptures and their exposition had served to set before the assembly the actions of God that had called it into being. And this led into the corporate response of thanksgiving and self-oblation in Christ, culminating in Communion. During the Middle Ages, as the whole Mass came to be regarded as an allegorical representation of Calvary, the assembly's role became that of spectator and the response of the layman perforce a private one, as he worships Christ in the Sacrament.

To give but one example, from Amalar's *De ecclesiasticis officiis*:[2]

> The deacons who stand behind the celebrant are a type of the Apostles who hid themselves in fear. The subdeacons who stand opposite the celebrant on the other side of the open altar are types of the holy women who remained standing near the Cross. The prayer after the consecration signifies the Passion of our Lord on the Cross. When the priest bows down (at the *Supplices*), our Lord bows His head and dies. The slight lifting of the voice at *Nobis quoque* refers to the centurion's loud profession at the death of Jesus. The deacons at this point straighten up and begin to busy themselves with the Body of the Lord, to signify the steadfast courage which seized the women and their work at the grave. At the concluding doxology the celebrant and the deacon elevate the Host and the Chalice and then set them down again, to signify Nicodemus' and Joseph of Arimathea's taking down our Lord's corpse from the Cross.

This allegorical theology reached its culmination in Durandus' *Rationale divinorum officiorum* which was in use till modern times, as is the commentary of Nicholas Cabasilas in the Eastern Church.

The Reformers were more deeply influenced by this allegorical understanding of the liturgy than appears on the surface. While they insist on the ministry of the Word by restoring the reading of the Bible and by taking over from the friars the extra-liturgical sermon, they see the two ministries of Word and Sacrament as essentially parallel, the one setting out in words and the other in actions the saving work of God. The response to both is an individual one. It is not surprising that the extremists practically abandon the sacraments as unnecessary, and retain and exalt the sermon alone in the regular Sunday worship of Christians. Those who, more faithful to Dominical institution, try to retain the Eucharist, tend to see it (as their immediate predecessors did) as a drama, and insist on the 'breaking of bread' and the 'pouring of wine' as the symbolic setting forth of Calvary to arouse the individual faith of the Christian.

If the text and the theological interpretation of the text can be as loosely associated as these examples seem to indicate, it may be asked on what grounds worship is indeed central to theological enterprise. Is there any real substance to the assertion *lex orandi, lex credendi*? Theological understanding appears almost to float free, responding to the needs and pressures of particular times and places, while the texts of the liturgy exercise little control over even the most fantastic flights of interpretation. And the more ancient and authoritative the liturgical text, the more it is frozen and apparently unalterable, the more susceptible it seems to be to variety of understanding. At the most it provides a point of original reference, a place to return to when a particular tradition of interpretation has run dry and no longer serves.

Certainly this was the case in the first period of the liturgical movement in the Roman Catholic and Anglican Churches in the first half of the twentieth century. Dom Lambert Beauduin and his disciples and imitators in the Church of Rome, and later also in the Church of England, notably Father Gabriel Hebert, read their own theology of Eucharist and Church into the texts of the Roman Mass and the Book of Common Prayer respectively. It would hardly be an oversimplification to describe both these texts, on an unbiased reading, as primarily concerned, in ways characteristic of their times, with the atoning work of Christ. The Canon of the Mass is a prayer of thanksgiving, focused on the oblation of the elements, and medieval interpretation fastened to this an emphasis on the sacrificial death of Christ on the cross made efficaciously present in their consecration by the priest at the recitation of the words of institution. The Prayer Book is in this medieval tradition, though in reaction to this particular theology of atonement. It likewise emphasizes the atoning merits of Christ's sacrificial death on the cross, but believes their efficacy to be communicated to us by our eating and drinking the bread and wine by faith with thanksgiving.

The theologians of the liturgical movement placed the emphasis elsewhere. They were concerned to instil again into the Christian people a sense of belonging to a community, of 'being' the Church, in a characteristic phrase. And they wished to see that community offering itself in service to God and the world. Their theological themes are, not so much the atonement, but the incarnation and the Church, the Body of Christ, as the 'continuation' of the incarnation. The preface of Gabriel Hebert's *Liturgy and Society* sets the liturgical movement in the context of that search for Christian identity in an increasingly secularized world with which the ecumenical movement and the revival of biblical theology are also associated. It was an essentially Western European movement inspired by a vision of a renewed Christendom that had captured the imagination of some of the best minds of the day, among them Jacques Maritain and Gabriel Marcel in France, William Temple and T. S. Eliot in England.

Thus Father Hebert writes, 'It became necessary to envisage the condition of modern Europe, which, having lost the common faith by which once it lived, is seeing its social life lose its cohesion and threaten to disintegrate altogether. One must ask whether the Church does not show the way, the only way, to the recovery of a common faith and a true social life'. (p. 8) So he set out to combat the common view that 'a man's religious beliefs are his private concern'. The consequence of this is that 'social life is left without a religious basis; the results are apparent in the disintegration of modern life'. (p. 17) 'While personal devotion is the mainspring of all Christian life, we lose hold of the essence of Christianity if we interpret it simply as a way of holiness, having for its end the salvation and the perfection of the individual soul. Personal religion, so interpreted, becomes a way of escape from the body by meditation and contemplation. But Christianity is the redemption of the body, and of common life, by the Divine action in the Incarnation. The Christian way of salvation through Christ is salvation in the mystical Body of Christ, the Church; and the Church, while it is not *of* the world, is *in* the world.' And, he goes on, 'it is clear that it is the function of the Church's Liturgy to interpret and express her life, and to exhibit the aim and meaning of human life in the light of the Incarnation'. (pp. 158–9) Bringing this down to earth, Father Hebert summarized the argument of his book in these words: 'the nature of the Church is seen most clearly in her sacramental order and her common worship: if this be so, we shall expect to learn in the actual visible Church of today and in the worship and life of our own parish Church the secret of God's meaning both for His world and for our little lives.' (p. 258) 'If on every Sunday in every parish Church the central act of worship were the eucharistic liturgy with the communion of the people, as in the early Church, that service would proclaim to the world what Christianity is.' (p. 165) Typical of this eucharistic theology was its emphasis on the offertory. The Church 'offers up to God the offering of the whole creation symbolized in the oblation of bread and wine, which includes the will of each member who shares in it to offer up his own life to God.' (pp. 207–8)

It is in this light that we can understand the insistence of the teachers of the liturgical movement on hearing and understanding the lessons at the Eucharist, and the introduction of the liturgical sermon. And hence above all their emphasis on 'communicating attendance'. The offertory procession is a particularly striking innovation in the case of the Prayer Book service of Holy Communion. Cranmer had omitted all mention of the offertory as 'stinking of oblation', and the interpretation of 'oblations' in the phrase 'alms and oblations' in the Prayer for the Church as referring to the elements is of course a later gloss. This is the period of missals with the text of the Latin and the vernacular in parallel, of people's service books with explanatory notes and pictures for children, of spoken commentaries from the pulpit during the service, and of 'para-liturgies' all but supplanting the originals, which are felt more and more to be intractable.

I have called this the first period of the liturgical movement in the twentieth century, for in it, in spite of new theological interpretation, both Roman and Anglican churches remained faithful to the recitation of their traditional texts. But the manner of recitation, the context, was changing – the music; the architectural setting, both in church buildings and in the widespread practice of domestic celebrations; above all the style of worship, expressive of deeply felt convictions. The posture of the officiant, the inflection of his voice when addressing the congregation, their own increasing readiness to acknowledge one another, all these betray an important shift in meaning. Up to this point the churches had contented themselves with what may be termed a 'theology of rubrics'. And rubrics are the province of the clergy, not of the people, who may feel deeply and protest at being asked to play 'Christmas games', as in 1549, or arraign a bishop for lighting candles on the Holy Table, as in 1889. But all to no avail. What was *done* at the liturgy was altered, and altered significantly, while what was said, though it might be used selectively, was left unchanged. The texts remained sacrosanct, and in principle at any rate susceptible to different interpretation, both to dissenters from the prevailing fashion, and at some future date to the Church as a whole. It required an exceptional consensus, or a clerical *coup d'état*, to overthrow the texts themselves so that they came into line with the developing theology of the rubrics.

But text and context are complementary, and pressure was mounting, pressure not only to do but to say what we mean, to read the lessons in the vernacular, to speak the canon aloud, and therefore naturally also in the language of the people, to compose appropriate prayers for the offertory, and to revive the *Pax*. Above all to say in the eucharistic prayer, not what our forefathers said, but what we ourselves feel the need to say. As Father Hebert put it: 'if Christianity is the redemption of all life, the things done and said in church must have a direct relation to the things done and said everywhere else; the sacraments and the liturgy exist in order to give to human life its true direction in relation to God, and to bind men in fellowship with one another.' (p. 8)

But what are we to say in our new liturgies, and how are we to say it?

Father Hebert looked for 'the recovery of a common faith to integrate again the social and political life of Europe'. It is strange now to look back, at a time when European concerns seem so domestic, to a generation when the renewal of 'Christendom', a European Christian civilization, was the hope of the best

Christian thinkers and men of imagination. The tacit assumptions of European superiority, the lack of knowledge of other world religions, and the consequent underrating of the pluralism of the modern world, now make much of their writing seem extraordinarily dated; and we are not wrong to detect an element of nostalgia that distorts their vision.

There is however one important factor which Father Hebert and his contemporaries recognized. They knew how deeply the Christian liturgy was interwoven with, and depended for its vitality on, the images and languages of Europe, on the resonance it sets up at every level, conscious and unconscious, in the worshippers who use it. It is a corporate, a social, work of art; and while a living work of art might be retouched, restored, added to, developed, it takes more even than a rare genius to recreate such a work *de novo*, for such a genius would have to be the spokesman of a vital culture.

It was therefore in a proper spirit of modesty that Father Hebert wrote that 'the forms of prayer which best meet the needs of the modern world are those which are most truly universal . . . and some of the oldest are those which are most truly modern'. (p. 226) That is a prescription to which the authors of the new liturgies have tried to be faithful, on the whole modelling themselves on the liturgically creative Patristic period. But the difficulty of this enterprise is formidable, and not only or indeed principally, because the imaginary and metaphorical vitality of the European languages is at present at a low ebb. The difficulty has more to do with the divorce of theology from liturgical texts, other than hymns. As we have seen, the theological self-understanding of the Christian community has for generations had to confine itself to the non-verbal aspects of public worship. Theology is out of practice, and will have to be recalled to a task from which it has long been banished, and to which it may be reluctant to return.

If therefore, after these reflections, we ask again how worship and theology are related, the answer will show that the health of both, and the health of the Church at the heart of whose self-understanding they are, has suffered in so far as they have been allowed to grow apart. For then the community and its story become separated and lose the means to enrich one another. If the text of the liturgy is allowed to become remote from the understanding of the contemporary Church, if it assumes itself the character of a sacred text (illegitimately so, for it is not part of the canonical Scriptures), then it freezes the particular theological understanding of its original era and ceases to be available to the living Church of later ages. We can no longer directly enter into the fullness of our story and have to make do with peripheral tales. And it is then that theology floats free, no longer earthed in the prayer of the people of God. Creeds and codes of behaviour harden and become lifeless, for the story-teller has lost his hearers, and they lose the story. Only together can worship and theology be the place of interpretation, where our world can find and work out the truth as it is appropriately learned and lived today.

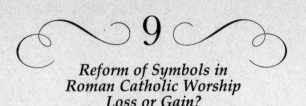

9

Reform of Symbols in Roman Catholic Worship Loss or Gain?

BALTHASAR FISCHER

During the years – nearly two decades – since the promulgation on 4 December 1963 of the Constitution of the Second Vatican Council on the Liturgy it has become almost a cliché, both within and outside the Catholic Church, to criticize the reform then introduced as being virtually untouched by the latest discoveries in the human sciences as to the significance of 'non-verbal communication'. Indeed, it is regarded as having led, on the whole, to an impoverishment of Catholic liturgy by a curtailment of the language of symbol, a curtailment dictated by latent rationalism. What had once been the crowning glory of Catholic liturgy – this is not infrequently the view of thoughtful Christians even of Reformed Church traditions – is said in this respect to have been, not perhaps destroyed, but certainly severely impaired by the zeal of sophisticated twentieth-century Catholics.

It is the responsibility of the academic (in our case, of the liturgist) to check the degree of truth in such wholesale judgements, without fear or favour. This essay therefore sets out to ask: has the reform of liturgical symbolic language which has taken place as a result of this century's post-conciliar reform of Catholic liturgy really, taking everything into consideration, resulted in the loss for which many people are blaming it? Or is it, perhaps, on the contrary true, as is claimed by the creators of this reform (among whom the present author must include himself), that on a closer and fairer examination we find indeed that the element of non-verbal communication has essentially been enhanced by the reform?

This article defends the latter position, the author, as one of the 'accused', duly acknowledging the twofold burden of proof which he has taken upon himself. One thing he must admit to straightaway with a heavy heart: the use made by the 'consumers' of the reformed Catholic liturgy is often in practice characterized by serious deprivation in the area of symbol-language. But a liturgical reform cannot fairly be blamed for everything that is made of it – often in defiance of its declared intentions. In this matter we can only hope that, with the general move, prevalent since the early seventies, away from the hostility to symbolism which marked the rationalistic sixties, the true intentions of the reform will find their proper expression in worship as it is celebrated in practice. Then the cliché about the symbol-language of Catholic worship having been distorted if not actually destroyed will gradually become impossible to repeat.

Our thesis (which may sound almost perverse against the background of the apparent state of Catholic liturgy after the Council) is that, through its latest reordering, Catholic liturgy has been enriched in the area of symbolic expression; and we shall defend it in three stages. We see enrichment achieved through lightening of a burden (I); through streamlining (II); and above all through restorations and even innovations (III).

I
Enrichment through Lightening of a Burden

To start with a particularly illuminating example from the eucharistic liturgy: since the early Middle Ages it had been the custom, during the concluding doxology of the Canon, to make the sign of the cross with the host three times over the chalice and three times between the chalice and the edge of the altar. The complete omission, at the reform, of this sixfold signing, which could in the last analysis only be interpreted by resort to allegory, must surely be seen as the removal of a burden. How this usage could work out and could appear, depending on the celebrant's temperament and sense of rhythm, in the late Middle Ages, may be inferred from the irreverent joke about the 'dancing God' which was current in fifteenth-century England.[1]

In the rules on the liturgical dress of bishops at the Pontifical

High Mass a very ancient symbol has been abandoned. To show that the bishop possesses the fullness of office within the Church he wore beneath his chasuble at the celebration of the Eucharist both the dalmatic of the deacon and the tunicle of the sub-deacon[2] – even in the height of summer, even in a tropical climate (though, admittedly, light silk tunicles and dalmatics were held in readiness if possible!). The abandonment, at the latest reform, of this sign – only visible to the bishop himself and to his immediate entourage – must surely be regarded as a lightening of the burden in the most literal sense.

At baptism, the administration of salt to the candidate – a custom certainly of venerable antiquity – has been dropped: but had this act not already become an example of those symbols (by no means rare) that once had been significant but had in the course of centuries degenerated into incomprehensible ciphers? The cipher may indeed finally take on meaning after an elaborate explanation by the celebrant (this is the occasion for the 'epiphany-experience', the 'Aha!-sensation', an effect much beloved of pastors who want to defend the retention of rites of this kind). But should not a liturgical action speak for itself, even if only allusively, if it is to reach not the intellect but the subconscious?

Also dropped from baptism, among other things, is the blowing on the candidate at the first exorcism. In this case we have an archaic exorcistic ceremony which modern people can hardly be expected to share in, so uncannily obvious is its meaning: frightening away Satan by blowing! The blowing could not have survived in any case, since the occasion for it, the imprecatory exorcism '*Exi ab eo Satana*', had to be abandoned because it was so likely to cause misunderstanding (apparent confusion of catechumens with the possessed). The reformed baptismal rite has not given up exorcism altogether (as has been falsely stated); but it now contains only the deprecatory exorcism, addressed not to Satan but to God, asking him to free the candidate from the power of the devil – and doing so only once, not, as previously, at three points in the service.[3]

A similar situation obtains with the slap on the cheek at confirmation. Here we must add that the universally popular pious interpretation of this as a knightly dubbing was untrue. This rite, first taken into the Roman Pontifical by a circuitous route *via* the Pontifical of Durandus of Mende († 1296), may have been a gesture originating in medieval secular custom used to signalize critical turning-points or transitions in young people's lives – such as the transition from the status of an apprentice to that of a journeyman. In this case too, where a symbol has lost its power to communicate and can only be made meaningful by academic interpretation, its removal means a lightening of a burden.

At the ordination of priests there have disappeared, among other things, the rites after communion, including the second imposition of hands. After they had been recognized (not least as a result of the pioneering researches of Bruno Kleinheyer[4] into the origins of the rite for the ordering of priests) as a decadent development, obscuring what originally was the essential, the one and only sacramental imposition of hands, their abolition had to be regarded as a notable lightening of the burden of the rite.

In the 1977 rite for the dedication of churches the traditional mass of ritual actions, which grew up not in Rome but this side of the Alps, was treated with remarkable gentleness and conservatism. Among major ritual elements there has been omitted only the symbol of the Latin and Greek alphabets written in a path of ashes diagonally across the church. Here also an academic explanation was required to make the rite comprehensible: this was once the way in which Roman surveyors symbolically expressed the conveyance of a property.[5] Granted that it may be painful for older people recalling earlier church dedications they had seen to miss this mysterious and solemn rite: but must the Church insist on its retention for young worshippers although they would look on astonished and bewildered while a bishop writes letters on the floor with his crozier as he walks through the church to be dedicated?

II
Enrichment through Streamlining

At a number of other points, gestures and signs long established have not simply been done away with, but streamlined by limiting their frequency, e.g. at the mass, in genuflections, and kissing of the altar. Anyone who remembers experiencing the old order as a celebrant will appreciate how the meaning of genuflection was spoiled by excessive frequency. The kissing of the altar had become so repetitive (before each turning toward the people) that the original function of this gesture, as a greeting to the altar and a bidding it farewell, had been lost to sight. Streamlining has achieved this much: there is now only one kiss to greet the altar, one to bid it farewell.

Streamlining is also to be observed in the reduction of the number of anointings in the sacrament of the sick (which has now had its proper title of *unctio infirmorum* restored). The custom of anointing the five senses as 'entry-points for sin' with a formula directed to the forgiveness of sins had resulted from an exclusive stress on one secondary effect of the anointing of the sick, the forgiveness of sins. This exclusive stress was, however, in its turn the result of the unfortunate shift in function of the sacrament itself into being a sacrament of the dying. In the immediate expectation of death the effect to which the biblical evidence (Jas. 5.15) and the new sacramental formula give precedence, the raising up of the seriously ill person, will inevitably be played on. It would have been possible to provide in the new procedure an act restricted to the anointing of the forehead (as may indeed be done in emergency); and if the reform had really lost sympathy with symbolism it would have rested content with this minimum. In fact, however, the reformed rite attaches importance to the sick person's being anointed, in normal circumstances, on the forehead *and* on the palms of both hands: in this sacrament, particularly, the whole of man's bodily existence is addressed.

III

Enrichment with Rediscovered or New Symbols

Our third section brings us to a series of extremely significant measures which make it hard to understand how anyone can speak of the latest Catholic liturgical reform as having lost sympathy with symbolism. In all we have said up to now, the reader might have felt that this or that symbol could have been left alone despite the arguments brought forward, or that this or that streamlining was not compellingly necessary. The real proof of our thesis lies in what we have to say now. The most recent

Catholic liturgical reform has breathed new life into crippled symbols and even created new ones.

1 The Symbol of 'Congregation'

Even the outward appearance of the mass now expresses more clearly, because of one of the most obvious changes, the truth that the congregation gathered under the leadership of its president for worship, especially for eucharistic worship, is a symbol that God, present in this world, is gathering men about that table for the celebration of the sacrificial meal instituted by his Son. The post-conciliar instructions regard the *celebratio versus populum*, which had survived only in the patriarchal basilica of Rome, as being once again a possibility which should be available everywhere. The taking up of this permission was so widespread that people even got the impression that the Council had forbidden the old fashion of celebrating with the celebrant's back turned to the congregation and had made the facing of the people obligatory. This is not the case,[6] and cannot be the case; for the old position of the priest at the altar is and remains a meaningful symbol in its own right, a symbol of a shared approach to the one Lord. (By the same token, the cross-bearer always had his back to the other people in the procession.) None the less, it must be said that the position of the president at the Eucharist facing away from the people had been bound up with a fateful misunderstanding of the Mass as an act of the priest which the faithful merely 'attended', as the conventional expression so revealingly put it. The new symbol of the *celebratio versus populum* dispels this notion at a stroke. As soon as you go in you see at once that the priest is the president and father of the congregation gathered around the holy table of the Lord's Supper-room. In this case also the reform merely revived a meaningful symbol which survived in merely vestigial form.[7]

2 The Symbol of the 'Altar'

The new instructions do not only assume the free-standing altar with sufficient space for the celebrant to go round it, at which it is possible to celebrate facing the people; they establish the option of disencumbering the altar of cross and candles (but first of all of flowers!), which no longer have to stand on, but may now stand beside, the altar. Where the Council's intention is understood, the ancient and venerable symbol of the altar can again become visible in the midst of a Catholic church, as it was originally meant to be: the empty throne, such as faces the visitor in the basilica of S. Maria Maggiore in Rome, from the top of the mosaic in the apse, the so-called *Hetoimasia*,[8] the throne waiting for its Lord to take his place upon it.

Moreover, in the revised regulations relating to the altar one very ancient symbol is, if not totally abolished, at least left to the discretion of church builders – the interment of martyrs' relics in the *mensa* or in the *stipos* of the altar. It is still today an eloquent symbol to celebrate the Eucharist over the grave of a martyr who died 'with' his Master in the death which is celebrated at this spot; but this symbolism cannot survive the moment at which the previous universal requirement of burying relics in the altar-stone made it necessary to celebrate the Eucharist, not above a dead body, but over minute splinters of bone from such a body. Both by removing symbols or by giving liberty in their use symbols can be freed to show their meaning.

3   The Symbol of 'Bread'

Even before the Council it was often the subject of complaint that a mistaken reverence was leading to thinner and thinner hosts, to the point where they almost resembled rose-petals, an unfortunate development that was losing the symbolism of 'bread'. It is characteristic of the post-conciliar regulations in the domain of symbolic expression that a detail apparently so trivial should not be overlooked. The General Introduction to the Mass appeals expressly for 'more bread-like' hosts: an official interpretation goes on to speak expressly and in detail of permitted variations in size, thickness and colour.

4   The Symbol of 'Communion from the Chalice'

Among the revivals in the domain of symbolism brought to the Catholic Church by the Council, hardly any was so important and unexpected as the permission given in Article 55 of the Liturgy Constitution for the laity to communicate from the chalice – which had been in desuetude since the Middle Ages. This permission, limited at first, was like a door being opened by just a crack – but in the years following the Council this crack has got wider and wider, until it even gives room, under specified conditions, for a parish celebration at which all the laity who desire it may receive the chalice. No one should accuse a reform of being hostile to symbolism when that reform has restored to the Catholic Church, in the most intimate area of its eucharistic worship, that *plenitudo signi*[9] which had been lost through 'a sad mischance of the times'.[10]

5   The Symbol of Communion 'ex eodem sacrificio'

In the same area, that of communion, the Council commended a further symbol which, following the precedent of Benedict XIV, Pius XII himself had advocated in his Encyclical *Mediator Dei*,[11] the symbol which consists of the faithful receiving at their communion, so far as possible, hosts consecrated at this celebration,[12] and not (though this abuse has still not died out) hosts from the tabernacle, consecrated at a previous Mass. Where this counsel is taken seriously, by the principle of non-verbal communication, the feeling for eucharistic table-fellowship must be strengthened.

6   The Symbol of 'Breaking'

The post-conciliar regulations for the celebration of the Eucharist again provide expressly for the breaking of the host for the communicants when they are few in number. Thus the primitive symbolism which says 'that we who are many become one Body from the one Bread of life, that is Christ' (1 Cor. 10.17) once again becomes accessible.

7   The Symbol of 'The Greeting of Peace'

When the Missal of Pius V appeared, one of the most expressive of the eucharistic gestures of the people was already hopelessly distorted: the symbol of respect through the Kiss of Peace exchanged by the faithful before communion from earliest times (originally, in Rome, before the offertory) had been replaced by a substitute, the so-called *Pacificale* or Pax-brede, passed along the rows of worshippers for each to kiss. Here too the post-conciliar reforms freed the old symbol from its distortion in a discreet way – by encouragement, not by prescription – and incorporated a permissive recommendation of a genuine greeting of peace (its form to be determined by the Bishops' Conference) into the order of the Mass. This symbol alone has been brought up from the depths of oblivion and, wherever it has been adopted, has altered the face, indeed the whole atmosphere, of the eucharistic celebration. The horizontal dimension of the eucharistic mystery, so vitally important and for centuries so thoroughly forgotten, once again has a place where it can be expressed in symbol.

8   The Symbol of 'Concelebration'

The old Catholic way of proceeding when several priests were together, of providing each with his own altar for a so-called 'private' celebration – perhaps even at the same time as Mass for the people – was a destructive symbol. By being separated into many private Masses, often even going on at the same time, the *mysterium unionis* had been perverted into a *mysterium separationis*. The situation which developed in places where many Masses were said daily must have seemed scandalous. In this matter the reform brought forward and purified an ancient symbol, which had maintained a shadowy existence in the West solely in the setting of ordination but had never been lost in the East: concelebration. Now, when several priests are together, it is again possible, with the help of this symbol, to live out delightfully not only the unity of the priests with one another but the unity of priests and people.[13] The importance of this element of revivified symbolic language can hardly be exaggerated.

9   The Symbol of 'the Orante Attitude at Prayer'

One of the basic gestures of the celebrant which runs right through the eucharistic celebration, the so-called *Orante* position of the hands, had in the Missal of Pius V been subjected to regulation which can only be characterized as totally insensitive. Since exaggerated stretching out of the arms was deprecated (we see clearly here the influence of the new insistence on moderation, typical of the Renaissance ideal of life), it was decreed that this gesture should be made 'before the breast', and in such a way that the limits of the body's width and height should not be passed, and the palms of the hands were facing each other. The gesture of prayer resulting from an exact observance of this rule must be simply dismissed as meaningless. It is typical of the instructions of the reformed Missal that this rule is deleted and not replaced; they say simply that at the relevant place the priest extends his hands.[14] The understanding reader appreciates that this restores to its rightful place the ancient stance which goes back to the pictures of the *Oranti* in the catacombs, that of the hands held up and open in the form of a bowl, and which was once the stance of prayer for the laity also and is still so for Moslems. In this case the reform has rescued one of the greatest symbols of prayer in the history of the human race from its neglect – the empty hands held out before our divine partner. We need think only of the contrary gesture, that of the clenched fist,[15] to appreciate the many-sided character of this rediscovered primal gesture.

10 The Symbol of the 'Sealing' of the Candidate by Parents and Godparents as well as by the Priest

Of the many examples of new or rediscovered symbols in the domain of sacramental celebration, we note only two: one from the domain of baptism, one from that of penance and anointing of the sick. The inclusion of parents and godparents in the act which the Fathers called the 'sealing', the signing of the baptismal candidate's forehead (not now the breast as well) with the sign of the cross,[16] is without precedent in liturgical history. It is a happy 'invention' of the editors of the new rite of infant baptism, which has been enthusiastically adopted on all sides. Here we meet the classic case of an immediately understood symbol which calls for no explanation. Parents and godparents feel what this sign means. They affirm and implore the taking of their child into the possession of the one who died on this cross, and triumphed! A special gain from this innovation is that it links with baptism a family custom which, one hopes, is still widespread: the custom whereby a mother, especially, signs her baptized child on the forehead in ancient Christian fashion with the cross[17] before he goes to sleep, in order to 'seal' him, by the power of him of whom the sign speaks, against all evil.

11 The Symbol of 'Laying on of Hands'

In the two domains of penance and anointing of the sick, the symbol of the laying on of hands on the head of the penitent or the sick person, so expressive in these particular areas, had become distorted in the course of centuries. In the first case the damage was done by the general adoption of confession in the confessional, in which, on practical grounds, the imposition of hands (through the grill!) was impossible. The editors of the old *Rituale Romanum* were still aware of what was at stake, and with touching helplessness instructed the confessor to hold out his right hand from the confessional in the direction of the penitent, before absolution. Since the new order assumes the co-existence of and the possibility of choice between the confessional and the confession-room as the scene of penance, it can say: '. . . the priest extends his hands, or at least his right hand, over the head of the penitent . . .'[18]

At the anointing of the sick it may have been prudishness which caused the tacit abandonment of this gesture, originally so universal and so natural in this setting. After earlier revisions of the *Rituale Romanum* had decided on the extension of at least the right hand over the sick person[19] this reform has now fully restored the complete imposition of both hands at the anointing.[20] In the process there appears a noteworthy sensitiveness to the special character of symbol-language, in that in both cases the imposition of hands is to be silent – speaking, that is, entirely out of its own symbolic nature.

12   *The Symbol of 'The Word'*

We have deliberately left one symbol in the post-conciliar liturgy till last. It runs through all acts of worship, in contrast to the cases discussed above, and it is indeed the most spectacular: the symbol of the comprehensible word. In this setting we cannot deny that the liturgical word uttered in an alien cultic language has a symbolic character after its fashion: it was a symbol of the separateness of what worship was celebrating, its transcendence of every-day concerns. But this was open to the great objection that it is precisely the word which is given to humankind as a means not of concealment but of revelation, and that Christian worship most particularly is dominated by the principle of a message proclaimed, of drawing people into a shared understood prayer. Thus the introduction of the vernacular into the liturgy (which only a few die-hards regarded as the total abolition of Latin) restored to the liturgical word its proper symbolic character. It is significant that opposition to this, the most marked change in the external appearance of Catholic liturgy, has remained confined to small groups, however vociferously it may be professed. Opinion polls have always shown that it has been particularly the elderly, in whom a certain nostalgia for Latin would have been understandable, who were glad to be able at last to understand and offer as their own prayer what had throughout their lives been withheld from them by the veil of an alien cultic language.

Against the background which we have drawn, we can give a more confident and positive answer to the question in the title of this paper. The cliché that the most recent Catholic liturgical reform is hostile to symbolism is a sweeping judgement both superficial and unjustified, falsely blaming the reform for what many die-hards – regrettably – have made of it. Where the reform is carried out as it is meant to be, Catholic liturgy's wealth of non-verbal communication, so long a cause of just pride, will gain new vigour.

10

The Liturgical Use and Abuse of Patristics

PAUL BRADSHAW

Liturgists, like many others in the Church, have always been prone to look back to some supposed perfect age in the past and to attempt to recreate it – or more often a highly romanticized version of it – in their own times. For some the age has been that of the Reformation, for others it has been the medieval era, while in our own day the desire to get behind these times to the sources of Christian worship has led to the patristic period being singled out as the golden age of liturgy, and consequently all modern liturgical rites are to a considerable extent reconstructions of supposed primitive practice. But just what is this 'patristic liturgy' which it is desired to imitate? Which particular age is it that we have in mind?

If we are to judge from the structure and content of current revised liturgies of the different churches, and especially their eucharistic and initiatory rites, then in a large measure it appears to be the fourth and fifth centuries onwards which are seen as the classical period of liturgical development, since many of the features retained or restored in today's rites are first known to us in the liturgy of that time. But why single out this particular epoch? It does not represent the most primitive form of Christian worship, but is rather a liturgy in transition: the Church was in the process of struggling to come to terms with what can be described not unreasonably as the most fundamental change in the whole of its history – the union of Church and State which followed the triumph of Constantine. The floodgates had been opened, and converts – or more often the half-converted carrying with them their pagan inheritance – were pouring in, and this was exercising a profound influence upon the Church's worship. The size of congregations was dramatically increased, and consequently the scale and style of the performance of the liturgy was being modified in order to meet this: the hitherto largely domestic celebration was transformed into a much more formalized *cultus publicus*. The old initiatory and penitential disciplines were breaking down under the strain of this influx, and had to change in order to cope with a new situation; while the lower level of comprehension of the Christian faith (and commitment to its standards) attained by many of the new generations of churchgoers were leading to significant alterations in liturgical practices, among them the introduction of court ceremonial and of pagan terminology and ideas. At the same time the emergence of the sense of the numinous, the notion of awe, dread and unworthiness among worshippers led in turn to a decline in the frequency of the reception of communion, as the Church attempted to communicate with, and exercise some control over, these barbarian hordes.[1]

This period is, therefore, something of a surprising choice as a model for the worship of the latter part of the twentieth century, when numerically our congregations are tending to return to a pre-Constantinian size, and when for the first time we are beginning to emerge from our identification with a nominally Christian society. Perhaps it has been unconsciously favoured because there is a greater availability of texts and sources than is the case for the preceding centuries, which makes a more complete reconstruction possible; or perhaps the architects of the new liturgies actually believe that the model on which they are basing their offspring is not the practice of the fourth and fifth centuries but rather that of the first three hundred years of the Church's history. In reality, however, we know relatively little about the worship of this earlier period, certainly far less than we tend to think we do, and many of the conclusions which are made about it are simply the reading-back of the practices of later ages into this earlier time. We may of course be correct in so doing, but we cannot be certain that we are. One small example may illustrate our lack of knowledge in this area. It is generally stated as an unquestioned fact in the textbooks of liturgical history that it was a part of the earliest tradition of the Church for a psalm to be recited between the Epistle and the Gospel in the Eucharist, which came to be known later as the Gradual Psalm. However, when we take a closer look at our second- and third-century sources, we find that we have only one mention of psalms in connection with the Eucharist, and that is by Tertullian, and it is made in relation to a Montanist service: 'whether it be in the reading of the Scriptures, or in the chanting of psalms, or in the preaching of sermons, or in the offering up of prayers . . .'[2] This is a very uncertain foundation upon which to make any assertion about the Catholic practice of the day: it *may* have been the custom to include a psalm between the readings at that time, but it is only in fourth-century sources that we find an explicit reference to it.

The paucity of allusions to liturgical practices in writings of the second and third centuries inevitably means that much importance is attached to the document known as the *Apostolic Tradition* of Hippolytus, as being almost the only extant liturgical text to date from this period. It has consequently played a major part in the work of liturgical revision in recent decades. Nearly every single revised rite of all the major churches has been influenced to a greater or lesser degree by it, and in some cases the prayers in the modern services are little more than translations of the equivalent material from this source. This is the case, for example, with the second eucharistic prayer in the Roman Catholic Mass, with the third eucharistic prayer in the Alternative Service Book of the Church of England, and with the ordination prayer for bishops in both the Roman Catholic and American Episcopalian rites. Such extensive and uncritical use of this document might not be so questionable, if we really could be sure that the text as we have it did date from this early period and did represent what might be considered as mainstream practice of the time. We are, however, far from such certainty on both counts. It has to be remembered that we do not possess an original manuscript of the work, but that it has to be reconstructed from translations into Latin, Arabic, Ethiopic, Sahidic and Bohairic, and from the use made of it in various later church orders. This alone should make us wary of claiming that we know what Hippolytus wrote, but our caution should be the greater when we bear in mind that the oldest translation, the Latin, was probably not made until about the middle of the fourth century, while the oldest manuscript of that translation which we possess dates from about AD 500, and that all the other works which made use of the *Apostolic Tradition* similarly derive from the fourth century or later.

In 1950 Professor E. C. Ratcliff warned that:

> the elapse of some century and a half, if not longer, between
> the composition of *Apostolic Tradition* and the making of the
> oldest known version of the treatise provokes certain
> questions concerning the authenticity of the Greek text which
> the translator had before him. In particular, students of the
> early history of Christian worship are prompted to ask
> whether the text of the Anaphora underlying the Verona Latin
> translation was genuinely a document of the late second or
> early third century, transmitted without addition, subtraction,
> or other important change or modification, to the century
> following; or, on the other hand, whether it had been altered
> and reshaped in accordance with the ideas or fashions of a
> subsequent day.[3]

He then went on to examine its eucharistic prayer in some detail,
and reached the conclusion that:

> the Anaphora which commonly goes by the name of
> Hippolytus cannot be considered as his, or as belonging to his
> time. In its general arrangement, and in the nature of not the
> least important of its details, so far from conforming with the
> liturgical tradition of the late second century or early third, it
> rather conforms with that of the fourth. On the other hand, a
> considerable portion of it has every appearance of preserving a
> fragment of the pattern of the type of eucharistic prayer to
> which Justin and Irenaeus are witnesses. So coherent is the
> fragment, that we are led to suppose that the authentic
> unedited form of *Apostolic Tradition* exhibited the pattern in its
> entirety.[4]

The original pattern, according to Ratcliff, consisted of more
extensive thanksgiving for the work of creation and redemption,
the absence of any epiclesis, and the inclusion of a final
thanksgiving for the admission of the worshippers to the
worship of heaven, culminating in the singing of the *Sanctus*.
Though Ratcliff's theory received strong support from Canon A.
H. Couratin and Dr G. A. Michell,[5] such a radical reconstruction
did not appear convincing to many,[6] and it has been generally
ignored, except that it has left traces upon the form of the Series 2

eucharistic rite of the Church of England, where the *Benedictus qui venit* was transferred to the very end of the eucharistic prayer, apparently in readiness for a further stage of revision in which the *Sanctus* would join it there.[7] Nevertheless, to have dismissed this particular reconstruction is not thereby to have removed all doubts about the authenticity of the extant text, and scholars would do well to remember the comment made by a distinguished colleague of Ratcliff: 'he was nearly always wrong – but always *interestingly* wrong.' His theory may have been mistaken, but that is not to say that he was mistaken in challenging the reliability of the text not only of the eucharistic prayer but also of the whole document as being the unaltered work of Hippolytus, and since that time some other voices have also expressed their doubts. A. F. Walls, for example, has questioned whether the Latin version is as reliable a translation as is generally supposed, E. Segelberg has claimed to discern various strata overlying the original text of all three ordination prayers, and I have followed Ratcliff in querying the authenticity of the present form of the whole rite of ordination.[8]

Unfortunately such warnings have not yet been heeded by the majority of liturgical scholars or by those responsible for drawing up new rites, who have preferred to assume that what we have before us is substantially what Hippolytus wrote. One cannot help feeling, however, that such a judgement is not entirely uninfluenced, though no doubt unconsciously, by the desire to have at least one solid piece of rock on which to base a reconstruction amid the shifting morass of brief hints and obscure allusions which make up the liturgical evidence of the second and third centuries. Moreover, even if they are correct in thinking that those who laboriously copied out and transmitted Hippolytus' work through successive generations did so with strict regard for historical truth and without any concern for conformity to the practices of their own day, there still remains a doubt whether the liturgy of the *Apostolic Tradition* does genuinely represent what was actually happening in the author's own church in Rome or wherever it was composed (and the question of provenance cannot be regarded as conclusively settled), to say nothing of what other Christians elsewhere were doing in their worship. It may be that it does give a faithful picture of primitive practice in general, but we know enough of the variety of early customs to entertain some doubts as to how widespread any one form of liturgical usage might have been at that period; and it is equally possible that to some extent it expresses what one individual thought ought to be done in the liturgy, and not necessarily what his church was in reality doing (as also seems to be the case in the fourth-century *Apostolic Constitutions*), or alternatively what he thought had been done in the past and was no longer being observed. It would be ironical if in its search for an authentic primitive pattern the Church of today was actually reconstructing an aberration from early practice which through some quirk of history has managed to survive while the genuine mainstream tradition has largely been lost. The fact that extensive use was made of Hippolytus by other church orders, and considerable similarities to it can be found in many later rites, does not itself guarantee the fidelity of his work to early usage, since their compilers could have been as much misled by the document as scholars of today. It is conceivable, for example, that the anamnesis paragraph in the eucharistic prayer, which has been the cause of so much dispute in the liturgical revision of the Church of England, was not a universal feature of the early liturgy, but a peculiarity of Hippolytus' rite which was later copied elsewhere, as was suggested long ago by Gregory Dix.[9]

In any case, if the real purpose of the return to the patristic period as a liturgical model for today is to ensure that our practice is based upon the earliest customs of the Church, should we not be retracing our steps further than the end of the second century? The liturgy which was known to Justin and Hippolytus was not the liturgy which was known to Peter and Paul in the first century. The way in which the Eucharist was celebrated at Rome in the middle of the second century, for example, would have been barely recognizable to the apostles, to say nothing of the difference in the way in which it was understood: their communal evening *meal* had been transformed into an early morning *service*; the sevenfold action had been telescoped into the fourfold shape; and the whole rite was now prefaced with readings and prayers derived from the synagogue order, in place of the more informal verbal contributions which had accompanied the meal in their day. Hence if we wish to conform our worship to the most ancient traditions, then it is to the New

Testament pattern that we must turn. Indeed some Christian communities have begun to explore the eucharistic agape as an enrichment of their sacramental experience, and others have argued that the free form of their worship, with spontaneous contributions from any member of the congregation, reproduces the typical apostolic service, though perhaps they greatly overestimate the degree of chaotic informality which would have been found in a strongly liturgical tradition like Judaism (after all St Paul was critical of such excesses in Corinth and insisted that 'all things should be done decently and in order'): the charismatic is just as much prone as the ritualist to reading back what he wants to find in the past.

The Church in general, however, has stopped short of such developments. Perhaps the intimacy of a meal instead of the more formalized structure of a service is just something which we are not ready for, at least yet, in the renewal of our congregational life and worship. Perhaps also we are deterred by a sense of uncertainty as to what precisely the first-century Church did in its worship. It is true that the New Testament evidence is rather limited and that there is something of a 'tunnel period' at the end of that era which makes it difficult to trace the evolution of later liturgical practices back to their roots in any detail, but our ignorance here may not in fact be very much greater than it is in the succeeding centuries where such confident reconstructions have been attempted, and the work of recovery not as hopeless a task as it has seemed to some. As in the quest for the historical Jesus, we must be prepared to abandon the old supposed certainties and accept that we cannot know as much as we would like to do; but there is still much we can discover if we tackle it in a different manner, without the blinkers of earlier presuppositions, if, for example, we do not expect to find *the* apostolic liturgy but instead a wide pluriformity of practice, and especially if liturgical scholars will take seriously the findings of contemporary studies about Palestinian Judaism before AD 70, and give up reading back the practices of later Judaism or relying on the work of earlier generations of Jewish scholars.

In the light of all this, however, we may be tempted to ask if it is worth the effort. Is the search for the origins of Christian worship at best an irrelevant pastime, an absorbing hobby for the bored parish priest, and a fascinating field of speculation for the academic? Should we not ignore history in general, and the early period of the Church's growth in particular, and instead simply be concerned to create liturgy for today, rooted entirely in our contemporary experience of God and our response to the needs of the present age? Certainly there are some ecclesial groups, frequently, though not exclusively, those of a charismatic kind, which seem to be moving in this direction. But such an attitude is fundamentally mistaken. History can never be irrelevant to a living faith, for worship and theology do not begin *de novo* in each age, but development or change in thought and practice always arise out of what has gone before. Our beliefs and actions are moulded by the tradition which we have inherited. We may rightly question that tradition, we may seek to restore a better balance, a truer perspective, to reform what has become corrupt and to incorporate new understandings and insights, but the foundation on which we are working is always our own earlier experience and the experience of previous generations of believers. To comprehend the present, therefore, one has to comprehend the past, for our concept of worship is conditioned by what worship has meant to those who have preceded us. One has only to look at the Reformation to illustrate this point. In spite of the efforts of the Reformers to free themselves from the inheritance of the Middle Ages, many old assumptions about worship were unconsciously adopted as normative by those responsible for drawing up the new liturgies – the 'low' celebration, the clerical dominance, the individualism, and the strongly penitential tone, to name but a few.

There is, however, another reason why history is especially important to Christianity. Because the Christian faith is essentially historical, grounded in particular events in the past, the elements of continuity with that past are vital: once it becomes divorced from its roots, Christianity can easily cease to be Christianity. Again and again, therefore, we need to return to those roots to re-examine our practice in the light of the tradition of the Church, and especially of the formative years of the patristic period, not because our forefathers were incapable of error but because that offers us a different perspective from our own, and one which is nearer to the events from which our faith takes its origin. It is only from this vantage-point, only by constant reference to the past, only by checking our experience against that of those who first apprehended the Christ-event and sought the appropriate response to it in worship, that we can be helped to judge our continuing fidelity to the revelation of God in Christ. For that reason, however uncertain we may be of the details of what happened then, the study of the origins and early development of the Church's worship will always be of the most crucial concern to the liturgist. It is there, with the accretions of later ages stripped away, that he may learn what is, or should be, at the heart of truly Christian liturgy, and it would be a great tragedy if in our training of leaders of worship we were to produce generations who were skilled in the art of creating liturgical forms for the present but who knew nothing of the riches of the past. For, in the words of that noted scholar, Josef Jungmann, 'history is a precious corrective of mere speculation, of subjective hypotheses. True knowledge of our present liturgy is knowledge based on the solid rock of historical facts; it is by studying the past that we can best learn how to shape the future.'[10]

Moreover, there is perhaps yet one further reason why at this particular point in time the early period of the Church's life and worship should be thought worthy of careful study. As I have suggested earlier, the situation of the Church today is in many ways more analogous to that of the pre-Constantinian age than it is to any other era in its history: it is set much more 'over against' the world than it has ever been since that time, a minority group, and in some cases a persecuted minority, in a pagan environment; and it is searching for a form of worship appropriate to these circumstances. It is only natural, therefore, that it should look towards the relative simplicity, flexibility and informality of the primitive Church for this. But, no matter how similar the two situations appear to be, it cannot be stressed enough that they are by no means identical, and it is thus a great mistake if we attempt to act as though they were. There are wide differences, not least of culture, which make it impossible simply to transplant the liturgy of one age and expect it to be an effective vehicle for worship in another. Similarly, we cannot put the clock back and pretend that subsequent events have never happened. We are not the early Church facing situations and groping towards understanding for the first time; we are heirs to a long and varied tradition which has deeply coloured and shaped our thinking about worship and theology, and it is the whole of that tradition which we have inherited, and not just a selected portion of it which we happen to prefer. We cannot just ignore everything which has taken place in the history of the Church after the first few centuries.

Perhaps one example will serve to illustrate this. When the draft form of the Series 2 Eucharist was under consideration in the Church of England in 1966–7, there was much dispute about the precise wording of the anamnesis paragraph in the eucharistic prayer.[11] The Liturgical Commission originally proposed to include the phrase, 'we offer unto thee this bread and this cup', which, it said,

> does not assert the fully developed doctrine of the eucharistic sacrifice. It confines itself to the simple language used by Hippolytus, Irenaeus, and Justin; and it even goes back to New Testament times, for it is used by Clement too. The use of the phrase is in line with the Anglican appeal to antiquity.[12]

This, however, was unacceptable to many Evangelical Anglicans, not necessarily because they were unhappy with the eucharistic theology of the early Church, but because they were, quite understandably, unable to ignore the doctrinal water which had flowed under the liturgical bridge in the intervening centuries and had brought into association with that phrase a very different doctrine of the Eucharist from that held in primitive Chistianity. While Hippolytus' words might still be used by twentieth-century Anglicans, they now carried more than Hippolytus' meaning because of their subsequent history.

In any case, this is one point at which appeal to Christian antiquity is not particularly helpful. Historically speaking, the development of thinking about the eucharistic sacrifice grew from the theologically less important consideration of *our* offering towards the more central concern of *Christ's* offering,[13] but the earlier notion, having found expression in the eucharistic prayer, was not easily displaced, and has remained to encourage doctrinal distortion ever since. If, however, what we really want to say is that in the Eucharist we 'enter into the movement of his [Christ's] self-offering',[14] then the language of the early Church does not provide the ideal starting-point for this. In this respect we must take seriously criticisms like those made by Leslie Houlden and Tom Baker,[15] that contemporary liturgies are too archaeological, too concerned with the past and insufficiently sensitive to the movements of current theological thought. There is a widespread sort of 'liturgical fundamentalism' which believes that 'if it's primitive, it must be right', which thinks that 'renewal' means 'revival', and sees purity and perfection solely in terms of returning to what has gone before. But the past does not hold all the solutions to today's questions, and all too often it seems that the makers of modern rites have sought to restore the ancient pattern for its own sake, without adequate consideration as to whether it accords with the current theological climate, our own cultural situation, or present pastoral needs. A particular case in point seems to be the new Roman Catholic pattern of adult initiation, which closely follows the patristic model of the catechumenate with its attendant stages, but which already in some countries is being found not to fit the reality of how people actually come to Christ.

If we really wish to create Christian liturgy for our own time, there can be no simple retreat into the past. Indeed, is there not an illogicality in appealing to patristic principles against some development in doctrine or liturgy, when one of the cardinal features of the early Church was liturgical freedom, with all the variety which inevitably ensued from this? Perhaps, therefore, one of the best lessons we can learn from our study of the primitive period is that, whatever attempts were made to define and establish norms and conventions, liturgical practice broke through them all as it tried to respond to changing cultural patterns, pastoral needs, and theological trends.[16] Many such developments, viewed in retrospect, may not always have served the best interests of furthering the Christian gospel, but they seemed the right course to the Church at that time. For all our professed espousal of the principle of freedom in worship today, underneath there still lies firmly entrenched a belief in the sort of authority and uniformity which has only been characteristic of liturgical practice since the end of the Middle Ages. The continuing control and propagation of liturgies from the centre, in place of natural growth from the particular worshipping communities, is a symptom of this. As far as liturgical texts are concerned, we appear still to be undecided whether we want a guide-book or a rule-book. We have started to produce material which suggests the former, but in many cases still tend to continue to impose it in a manner which implies the latter.[17]

Nevertheless, just as we cannot rely exclusively upon what the Church has done before, so also we cannot blindly follow ephemeral theological fashions. Which particular theological school, for example, from the many which are current throughout the Church today is to be taken as normative? And is the theology expressed in our liturgies to be that of the theologian or of the man in the pew? We are faced with a bewildering range of options, which may partly be the reason why we have tended to retreat into the past. Quite clearly what is required is, in the popular jargon, some sort of 'creative tension' between adhering to tradition and following contemporary trends, in order to avoid the unacceptable extremes of either position. However, that is much more easily said than put into effect, and it has the danger of leading towards a terrifying anarchy. But we have to risk letting liturgy go wrong if it is to develop naturally at all, if it is to have any real chance of getting it right. For, in the end, the only real test of good liturgy is the test of time: what continues to provide an appropriate means of worship for a community genuinely seeking to respond to the revelation of God in Christ will survive, what does not will perish.

11

Liturgical Revision in the Church of England in Retrospect
COLIN BUCHANAN

So it is all over now. The liturgical captains and kings depart, the fuss dies down, the sense of continuous change is stilled (one nearly added, 'and the evening comes'), and, as suddenly as it began, textual revision of the liturgy in the Church of England is all over. No wonder the editor commissioned an 'epitaph'.[1]

It all began in the post-war era, and for the English-speaking Christians it began, as far as I can see, in South India (where English is a Christian *lingua franca*, but nowhere the vernacular). That was in 1950, when the second synod of the newly-born Church of South India accepted and authorized the eucharistic rite (The Liturgy of the Church of South India),[2] produced by the committee established by the first synod in 1948. The CSI Liturgy proved to be not only influenced by Gregory Dix (which it avowedly was),[3] but also seminal in its own right. And, whilst revisions of eucharistic liturgy in the Anglican Communion were still grinding on with 1928-type texts,[4] a trend was being set which the compilers of the CSI Liturgy could hardly have foreseen.

New texts reflect new moods, and England in the 1950s was seeing a new mood. The Parish Communion, so earnestly advocated by the pre-war *avant-garde*, had now become standard Anglican practice. And perhaps this change of mood was a cautious step towards that renewal of worship which was uppermost in the mind of many continental Roman Catholics, and was coming into their practice. But, whatever the problems of reforming Roman Catholics (and they looked fearsome in the 1950s), Anglicans were stuck with texts which were almost anti-Liturgical Movement in their ethos (yes, even the new ones which were based on 1928), and with no possible lead from the

Church of England where, quite apart from usual traditionalism – and a stalemate of churchmanship clashes – there existed no machinery in the 1950s to make any changes, even if the Church of England could have agreed what it wanted.

It was a happy chance that led the compilers of the CSI Liturgy to find a way back in to the Anglican scene, and it came through the person of Leslie Brown, and his role at the Lambeth Conference of 1958 and later in the compilation of *A Liturgy for Africa* (1964).[5] Dix had other followers also, not least Edward Ratcliff and Arthur Couratin on the Church of England scene. Thus the pressures towards a revision of eucharistic liturgy along certain lines became strong in this country – pressures in which there could be discerned the popular Parish Communion movement, driven along by Parish and People's publicity, allied with these insights of Dix, and bodied out by the particular scholarly bents of Ratcliff and Couratin.[6] A Liturgical Commission was appointed in 1955 (when it was thought there might soon be a change in the law which would allow of liturgical revision), and some expectations obviously attached to this body, for all that its initial years were whiled away in remote seclusion rather like a liturgical dons' dining-club. There is little need to go over the details again. The timetable of revision in the Church of England was dictated by the legal considerations,[7] but it bore an amazing resemblance to the timetables observed also by the Roman Catholic Church, by Anglicans overseas, and by the Free Churches in England. Essentially, English-language liturgical revision took place in two stages:

1 'Thou'-form texts, which ruled unchallenged until 1966, and yet never produced a new text after 1968

2 'You'-form texts, which were unthinkable before 1966, and invariable after 1968

This analysis can easily be verified for the Roman Catholic Church, for Anglicans round the world, and for, say, the Methodist Church of Great Britain.[8] There is a watershed between the two categories, and it can be fixed almost to the day. The existence of two categories can be seen from the standpoint of history as that which made the revision of texts an ongoing 'movement', and not just a single isolated event in each country or communion. Revision generated its own momentum, and, although the necessity for changing to addressing God as 'you' precipitated post-1968 revisions, yet the fact that a further round was occurring invited more thoroughgoing revision in all sorts of directions. Thus the 1970s saw texts which in various ways reacted against 'sexism' in texts and rubrics,[9] reconsidered the structure of the 'fourfold action', went for ever more flexibility and openness in the overall presentation of the rite,[10] and, for instance, explored the meaning of the Peace at greater depth.[11] Alongside this handling of the Eucharist came polishing and tidying of the calendar and lectionary, revision of daily offices and occasional services to match the main texts, and, sometimes, the exploration of situations for which traditionally no provision had been made.[12]

In the Church of England, a relatively slow start in the sixties led to a perceptible quickening in the early seventies – this last produced by a tightly controlled timetable by which all decisions in General Synod had to be taken by 1979 in order that the (now well-worn) ASB might be put into production for November 1980. The pressure was due to the synodical procedures, unique in the Christian world. In the early seventies, there existed a 'Liturgical Steering Committee' of General Synod, which took responsibility for seeing Series 3 Communion through the Synod. The Steering Committee had no power to alter the text itself – it merely had to respond to requests by Synod, or, when it had interviewed some would-be amender, to bring its own amendments to Synod. But the system came under censure from Synod when various instant amendments were carried at the first outing of Series 3, and the text was in danger of being disembowelled by snap votes without full debate, and without opportunity for redress after mature reflection.[13] So the Standing Committee in 1973 brought to Synod a change in standing orders, whereby there would be a 'Revision Committee'. Then the services ran (or limped) through Synod in the following stages:

1 Debate on 'General Consideration' – a seminar-type discussion, with no amendments, and (short of refusal to

'consider') no decisions.

2   Reference to the 'Revision Committee', which as a committee has power to amend the text, and does so as it receives suggestions and proposed amendments from any member of Synod (members have the right to appear before the committee, as well as to send it written amendments).

3   The Revision Stage in General Synod – where the amended text is tabled, but members of the Synod still have the power to propose further amendments in full Synod.[14] At the end of this stage, the Synod votes on 'provisional approval', usually by a show of hands only.

4   Reference to the House of Bishops – which has the power to propose the final form of the text to Synod, and thus can (and occasionally does[15]) amend the text which gained provisional approval before returning it to Synod.

5   The Final Approval Stage in General Synod – where in the 1970s no amendments could be taken to the text proposed by the House of Bishops, and where the requirements of the Worship and Doctrine Measure[16] are met by the Synod being counted by Houses, and services only gaining 'Final Approval' if they get a two-thirds majority in each House.

The upshot of this pattern was an ever-increasing number of sittings of the Revision Committees with every subsequent year that passed. The Synod flexed its powers of amending, and found them enormous. Granted such muscles, who could resist using them? As the services became thick and frequent, so the amendments submitted for each one to the Revision Committee advanced by a sort of geometrical progression. Had not an end been in sight from the beginning (or at least from February 1976),[17] who can tell who would have survived to tell this tale? When I myself wrote in July 1978 of 'the years which the Revision Committees have eaten', it was Geoffrey Cuming who echoed the sentiment most warmly. Consider then the synodical activity in connection with liturgy in 1977, to take but one year, as shown on the following list:

	Collects	Marriage	Calendar Lectionary	Ordination	Initiation
February	Final Approval	Completing Revision-Stage	General Consideration		
		with House of Bishops	with Revision Committee (15 full days of meetings from March to Sept.)		
July		Final Approval		General Consideration	
				with Revision Committee (6 full days of meetings in Sept. and Oct.)	
November			(Ready for Revision Stage but not on Agenda)	(Ready for Revision Stage but not on Agenda)	General Consideration
					with Revision Committee (6 full days of meetings in December and until the following March)

This list omits debates on the general concept of the Alternative Service Book and progress with it (February and November), a debate on the canons on Baptism (November), and a debate on the use of the Roman Catholic texts (November). But it indicates the great scope for putting in amendments which existed for ordinary members of the Synod, and the demands being made on the few for attendance at Revision Committees.[18]

So it was that, from all the ingredients thrust hastily into the synodical fires, stirred furiously by 550 members, and fashioned by the whim of man, and, so we trust, the overruling providence of God, there came out this Book. The history is recounted more objectively and less excerptively elsewhere. But it falls to my part to note something of the role of Geoffrey Cuming within it all – and this too will be excerptive, and certainly subjective.

Geoffrey first joined the Liturgical Commission after the triennial shake-up in 1965, and I first met him at St Katharine's Foundation in December of that year when the Commission convened after the appointments were made. I knew him as the scholar of *The Durham Book*, and the final lecturer – on the same Restoration period – in the tercentenary collection for the 1662 Prayer Book entitled *The English Prayer Book 1549–1662*. If the former book, his *magnum opus*, reflected his meticulously exact scholarship, then the latter illuminated splendidly his teaching ability to chart simple ways through complex material, and to deliver balanced judgements *sine ira et studio*. Encounter with Geoffrey in the flesh not only confirmed both these opinions, but has left me ever since muttering (by direct comparison with Richard Hooker) 'the judicious Dr Cuming'. Round the table of the Liturgical Commission he has brought diplomacy and humour (great gifts for puncturing the inflated and reconciling the polarized), and the sheer productiveness of the Commission has owed untold debts to these human qualities which he has harnessed to the Commission's labours.

From the start, his contributions to the output of the Commission were great in quantity, often unheralded or unnoticed in public, and always constructive and irenic in execution. Some vignettes of him as a liturgical scholar engaged in this very practical work may be of interest:

1   He had a big hand in the compilation (largely done in 1967) of the Commission's first 'modern language' proposals, *Modern Liturgical Texts*.[19] He drafted not only the Te Deum for this, but also (as is publicly acknowledged) the version of Series 2 Communion updated linguistically at the back of the Collection. In producing this he incidentally provided for the whole English-speaking world a 'new' Agnus Dei:

> Jesus, Lamb of God; have mercy on us.
> Jesus, bearer of our sins; have mercy on us.
> Jesus, redeemer of the world; give us your peace.[20]

2   In 1969 there was published the first edition of his *A History of Anglican Liturgy*, which not only replaced Procter and Frere, but was a model of historical writing on liturgy – a true *multum in parvo*. (The second edition came in 1982).

3   In 1972 Douglas Harrison resigned from the Commission and ceased to be vice-chairman. This position Geoffrey then took up. He rarely had to exercise it, as Ronald Jasper hardly missed a session since the beginning of all things in 1955. But

when he did, his care for a common mind and true accord has come through. The appointment – semi-official though I think it was – reflected the respect for Geoffrey's integrity which marked the whole Commission.

4   In his years at Humberstone, after St John's College first came to Nottingham, I asked him in three successive years to come and give a lecture on the University and College graduate course in liturgy here. He simply fitted in with the syllabus wherever it had reached for the day he was free to come. So I heard him lecture on the '1927–1928 Prayer-Book', on 'Landmarks in the Liturgical Movement in the Church of England', and on 'Church Architecture' (including tips on getting rid of pews). All were marked by his economy and precision with words, his ability to unearth material others might not have found, and his skill in weaving the known and the unknown into a consistent pattern for presentation.

5   In 1973 the Commission worked on *The Eucharist Today*, a symposium on Series 3 Communion. Geoffrey was allocated a chapter on 'A Structural Comparison with 1662', and here he displays himself again as a model of clarity and simplicity, even when 'pushing' a new idea, and as a mine of recondite information.

6   In 1975, Geoffrey became a member of General Synod, elected to the London University seat once held by Ronald Jasper before him.[21] Immediately he found himself on those interminable Revision Committees, and at intervals he chaired the 'steering' committee which presented the Revision Committee's proposals to Synod.[22]

7   Some of his best work on a synodical committee must have been on the dreaded Calendar and Lectionary Revision Committee in 1977. His patient care for historical accuracy and rubrical detail can rarely have had a better chance for deployment.

And so we begin the era of the new Book. As Anglicans we lag behind the Americans[23] and the Australians.[24] So there is opportunity, in looking at the effects of a new Book in those

Anglican churches, for us to learn what happens in the years following the introduction of a book. But there are also features of the Church of England scene which will be unique and will not mirror anything anywhere else. Writing some six weeks after the launching day of 10 November 1980, I discern the following trends:

1   We are still involved in a heavy confrontation with lovers of the Book of Common Prayer (and particularly its language). Their position is from one point of view guaranteed by the law of the land, which requires the BCP to be still available, and gives PCCs the right to choose which they use. But the lovers of the ancient take the view that a weighty publicity campaign is actually imposing modern-language services on those who do not want them, and a certain divisiveness has occurred and will not easily go away.[25]

2   Even for those who have been using Series 3 booklets, there is still a transition to come. Many parishes may be slow to equip their pews with ASBs, and many are remaining with little booklets (and thus, for instance, with 'time of trial' in the Lord's Prayer), and the speed of changeover cannot be hurried. Thus there may actually be greater confusion for the next two or three years than there has been over the last ten! But it will be confusion which will always be moving towards a solution, like a half-done jigsaw puzzle.

3   There is a rash of literature and other multi-media materials to accompany and explain the ASB. This includes commentaries,[26] books of prayers, suggestions for use of hymnody, guidance for music to accompany the Eucharist, and even help with episcopal ceremonial.[27] I have had my own share in this explosive growth industry (one of the very few growth industries in England in 1980), and cannot therefore *regret* it. Indeed, I think the general bubble and excitement is very good for the Church, so long as one bears in mind that it may make little difference to what a particular parish service *feels* like. Sunday worship should benefit from the fullness of provision in the Book, and from a growing understanding of Anglican worship by the worshipper. But it will not in itself necessarily be altered much by the coming of

the ASB.

4   We have still not reached a full conjunction of Catholics and Evangelicals, though we do now have texts largely agreed between them. There are some signs of a genuine convergence; Catholics have to reckon with truly reformed features of Roman Catholic worship, and that has done them good; and Evangelicals have found themselves positively sacramentalist as they have lost their paranoia in the Church of England. But the doctrinal conjunction has not happened in the way one could have hoped – partly because the issues of the day (especially the ordination of women) have proved both preoccupying and disruptive. But whilst joint texts enable us to worship together, they also should promote true theological dialogue and mutual reformation. We are still some way off this.[28]

5   There will be further liturgical texts of a supplementary sort to come during the 1980s. These will not threaten the position of the ASB, but they may enrich its provision. As I write the Commission's proposals for services for the sick have just been published, and will have their first run in General Synod in July 1981.[29] And when a new Commission is appointed it may have other supplementary tasks to do. Indeed it may itself be both 'coaching' in the use of the ASB, and, in a few years' time, gathering responses to the ASB.

6   There may be further steps to be taken to get the theologians and the liturgists into relationship with each other. There have been occasional, but persistent, noises to suggest that some theologians view the liturgists as Flat Earthers (or at least Three-Decker-Universers). Dare we nowadays talk about historical creation and historical fall? Or assert that Moses led his people out of Egypt across the Red Sea? Or venture to affirm more crucially that Jesus, both God and man, was conceived in the womb of a Virgin? Or even that he rose from the dead? The Commission was well aware of these questions, but was unable to see how the tradition could be overthrown for the sake of speculative answers to the questions. Some gentle trimming we did, but the radical solution we avoided – and not only because we thought the

traditional formulations important (however much they might then need interpreting), but also because we wholly failed to discern an alternative liturgical programme developing from the questioners. And that question remains – what do demythologized prayers and creeds and hymns look like? And what power can they convey? And what sort of tradition would *they* become?

7   But the best possible prospect is that worship will be, at the level of basic texts, taken for granted, so to speak, within the Church of England. There has been much corporate navel-gazing – but we now have some certainty about reasonably good health in the navel region. Perhaps we can flex our limbs, stretch our liturgical muscles, and develop our practice accordingly. The Church of England, bless it, gets so pre-occupied with texts, and we have given it all too much excuse to do so. Let us move on now to health-giving and creative practice.

So much for the future. Perhaps I could indulge myself in one last look back, and reveal a threefold nightmare about the might-have-been which sometimes afflicts me:

1   Just suppose the Church of England had had an official *hymnbook*, and had revised that in the way it has revised its services. Imagine the doctrine and the poetry all being revised line by line by majority votes in Synod. Think of the favourite hymns from all sides which would have been tabled for inclusion, and made the subject of debate and votes.

2   Just suppose that the Church of England had not hived off the Welsh dioceses to become the Church in Wales in 1920. Then, with the Welsh dioceses represented in Synod, it is certain that the whole project would have had to have been *bilingual* – right the way through to an ASB of 2500-odd pages! The committees would have been constantly assaulted by suggestions that nuances in the English had been lost in the Welsh, the Welsh text would have been the subject of amendments in Synod on which 98 per cent of the members would have been incompetent to vote, the backlash of the English-speaking dioceses would have wounded the Welsh-

speakers to the heart, and the task would have taken till 2000.

3   Just suppose (to pile Pelion on Ossa) that Gregory Dix had lived. Suppose his mischievous, maverick, learned perversity had been charming, beguiling and bewitching the Commission and all its works. How then would the course of revision have gone? For he would only be 79 years of age now . . .

But then there might be another nightmare also. Suppose we had had no Geoffrey Cuming over these last fifteen years . . . That would cause some real retrospective sweating. Thank God that by his providence we have been spared all four parts of this haunting nightmare!

12

The Work of Geoffrey Cuming

An Appreciation
DONALD GRAY

And still they gaz'd and still the wonder grew
That one small head could carry all he knew.

(Oliver Goldsmith, *The Deserted Village*)

It is true that Oliver Goldsmith was actually writing here of the schoolmaster of Auburn rather than the parson, but there are many of us who have had reason from time to time to stand amazed at the erudition and encyclopedic knowledge of Geoffrey Cuming.

Yet seldom could learning have been more lightly worn! No one hesitates to ask a question of Geoffrey lest in the asking the inquirer might be made to feel a fool for not knowing the answer; information is shared freely and generously with the enthusiasm of a teacher whose primary concern is to arouse a corresponding enthusiasm in his pupil. There is a whole generation of liturgical scholars in England who would want to acknowledge the encouragement and sheer practical help that Geoffrey Cuming has given them in pursuing their researches and studies.

This *Festschrift* eloquently bears witness to the international and ecumenical nature of Geoffrey Cuming's reputation as a scholar. And yet that reputation, celebrated here by a group of distinguished liturgists, has been mainly acquired in the classical tradition of the Anglican parish priest who quietly continues his studies amidst the daily concerns of his pastoral responsibilities. The bulk of Geoffrey Cuming's liturgical and historical work has not been done in the atmosphere of academia, but with the interrupting knock on the vicarage door always in prospect. Those of us who attempt but a pale imitation of a great tradition join our more single-minded academic brothers in saluting this present-day exemplar of the scholar-parson.

Geoffrey Cuming's achievements are varied. Not only are there his published works but also his less-publicized activities as lecturer and committee-man. This latter occupation is not held in high regard, particularly if that committee is concerned with producing material for the Church's worship. The Church of England has adopted a pose of great suspicion about the idea that a group of fifteen or sixteen men and women sitting around a table could ever produce a new liturgy. Some have spoken as if they preferred to await the advent of another Cranmer, heaven-born no doubt. Amongst the clergy this is in the main a pose, the truth being that the average clergyman is unwilling to admit that anyone can do the task better than he can!

In 1965 new appointments to the Liturgical Commission brought on to its membership both Geoffrey Cuming and another immensely able scholar-parson, Charles Whitaker, whose friendship as well as scholarship I venture to suggest Geoffrey would wish to be mentioned in this *Festschrift*. Perhaps only the PhDs of the twentieth and twenty-first centuries will reveal by the techniques of computer-based source-criticism the extent of the influence of these two most Anglican of scholars. Meanwhile let one eyewitness reveal that an enormous quantity of their labours is now enshrined in the pages of the Alternative Service Book. To be present at one of their drafting sessions was to attend a seminar of absorbing interest.

No one would expect that the bulk of the work of the Commission under Ronald Jasper was done in committee. Every meeting had to be prepared for by the composition of drafts and memoranda which could be the basis for intelligent discussion and debate. However, the Commission, while respecting the scholarship and the time-consuming labour which lay behind any submitted document, would more often than not send the draftsman back to modify his proposals in the light of the Commission's discussions. Geoffrey's work was no exception to this process, and he was always willing to submit cheerfully to its discipline, although he was a past-master of the technique of winning at the third or fourth round a battle apparently lost at the first. It is no coincidence that he was one of the first to be co-opted on to the new Liturgical Commission in 1981.

Geoffrey Cuming's published works are many and varied; a cursory glance at David Tripp's Bibliography will reveal him as music critic; as editor of *Studies in Church History* which are the published papers of the Ecclesiastical History Society; as a contributor to the deliberations of the Oxford Patristic Conferences; and also as a world authority on Anglican liturgy. His standing as a liturgical scholar will always guarantee him an attentive audience at any gathering of his peers. Geoffrey's contributions to the Congresses of *Societas Liturgica*, an international and ecumenical society formed in 1967, have been equally distinguished, and the *Societas* elected him to serve on its Council.

In recent years Geoffrey Cuming has shared the fears of those who have seen the study of liturgy becoming the Cinderella of the subjects taught in the Faculties of Theology of our universities and even in our theological colleges. At the time of his retirement from a lectureship at King's College, London, in the summer of 1980, he was one of the few university lecturers in England specializing in liturgical subjects. It was in order to encourage those who were teaching liturgy in various academic establishments, and like-minded parish clergy, that he suggested the formation of a Society for Liturgical Study which has already had three successful conferences: in 1978 at Mount St Bernard Abbey, in 1980 at St Deiniol's Library, Hawarden, and in 1981 at Spode House. It was only appropriate that at the first of these conferences Geoffrey was invited to give the inaugural 'Patriarchal' lecture (which is to be a feature of each conference), to the evident delight of all present.

Thus I return to the theme of Geoffrey Cuming's kind and painstaking encouragement of younger scholars, testimony of which can be read in the 'acknowledgements' in many recent works of liturgical scholarship. The Collections of the Alcuin Club (he has been a member of its committee for a number of years) are a fruitful source of these genuinely-felt expressions of gratitude. The high repute of the contributors to this *Festschrift* is sufficient testimony to Geoffrey Cuming's standing in his major field of study.

The Church of England ought to be proud that this latest member of a notable succession of scholar-parsons should attract such distinguished academic acclaim. We know that the subject of this special and loving recognition will accept it with characteristic shyness – and slight incredulity.

A SELECT BIBLIOGRAPHY
(excluding reviews)
Compiled by David Tripp

1 *As Author or Contributor*

'Mozart's Oboe Concerto for Farlendis', in *Music and Letters*, vol. xxi (1940), no. 1 (January), pp. 18–22.

'The Jews in the Fourth Gospel', in *Expository Times*, vol. lx (1949), pp. 290–2.

'Haydn: Where to begin', in *Music and Letters*, vol. xxx (1949), no. 4 (October), pp. 364–75.

'The Text of "Messiah"', in *Music and Letters*, vol. xxxi (1950), no. 3 (July), pp. 226–30.

'Advent and the Prayer Book', in *Theology*, vol. liv (1951), no. 378 (December), pp. 449–55.

(with Francis F. Clough): *The World's Encyclopaedia of Recorded Music*. London, Sidgwick and Jackson, in association with the Decca Record Co., 1952. Also USA, London Gramophone Corporation, 1952, 1966; Newport, Conn. 1970.

'The Making of the Durham Book', in *Journal of Ecclesiastical History*, vol. vi (1955), pp. 60–72.

(letter to the editor on) 'The Baptismal Interrogations', in *Theology*, vol. lix (1956), no. 431 (May), pp. 202–3.

'The Prayer Book in Convocation, November 1661', in *Journal of Ecclesiastical History*, vol. viii (1957), no. 2 (October), pp. 182–92.

'The Grand Debate', in *Church Quarterly Review*, vol. clxiii (1962), pp. 29–39.

'The Making of the Prayer Book of 1662' = pp. 82–110 in A. M. Ramsey and others, *The English Prayer Book 1549–1662*. London, SPCK 1963.

(with F. F. Clough): Appendix Four: List of Recordings [of music by Ralph Vaughan Williams] in M. Kennedy, *The Works of Ralph Vaughan Williams*. London, OUP 1964.

'Two Fragments of a Lost Liturgy?', in G. J. Cuming, ed., *Studies in Church History*, vol. iii (Leiden, E. J. Brill 1966) pp. 247–53.

'The English Rite: "We offer this Bread and this Cup": 4', in *Theology*, vol. lxix (1966), no. 556 (October), pp. 447–52.

(anonymous author of): modern English version of Series 2 Holy Communion, printed as Appendix: The Holy Communion (pp. 43–53) in Church of England Liturgical Commission: *Modern Liturgical Texts*. London, SPCK 1968.

A History of Anglican Liturgy. London, Macmillan 1969.

'The Liturgical Way Ahead', in *English Church Music* (1971), pp. 9–16.

(articles in) J. G. Davies, ed., *A Dictionary of Liturgy and Worship*

(London, SCM 1972), Books, Liturgical = 4, Anglican (pp. 82–4); Churching of Women (p. 137), Commination (p. 142); Matrimony = 4. Anglican (p. 259); Sick, Visitation of the (pp. 347–49).

(letter to the editor on) 'The New Moralism', in *Theology*, vol. lxxv (1972), no. 621 (March), p. 148.

'La base néotestamentaire de la prière commune', in *La Maison-Dieu*, 116 (1973), pp. 19–40. English original in *Studia Liturgica* 1974; Dutch version in *Ronde Tafel*.

'The New Testament Foundation for Common Prayer', in *Studia Liturgica*, vol. x (1974), pp. 88–105.

'Series 3 and 1662: a Structural Comparison', in R. C. D. Jasper, ed. *The Eucharist Today. Studies on Series 3* (London, SPCK 1974), pp. 34–45.

'Egyptian Elements in the Jerusalem Liturgy', in *Journal of Theological Studies*, N.S. vol. xxv (1974), no. 1 (April), pp. 117–24.

'Service-Endings in the Epistles', in *New Testament Studies*, vol. 22 (1975), pp. 110–113.

(with R. C. D. Jasper, tr. and ed.) *Prayers of the Eucharist, Early and Reformed*. London, Collins 1975.

'Eastern Liturgies and Anglican Divines', in G. J. Cuming, ed., *Studies in Church History*, vol. 13 (London, CUP 1976), pp. 231–8.

Hippolytus: A Text for Students; with Introduction, Translation, Commentary and Notes (*Grove Liturgical Studies*, no. 8). Bramcote, Notts, Grove Books, 1976.

(contributions to) C. Jones, G. Wainwright, E. Yarnold, eds., *The Study of Liturgy* (London, SPCK 1978): ch. 5: The Divine Office, 1: the first three centuries (pp. 353–7); ch. 5: The Divine Office, 6: The Office in the Church of England (pp. 390–5); a paragraph on the early Lutheran Office (p. 396).

'The Eucharist', in G. J. Cuming, ed., *Essays on Hippolytus* (*Grove Liturgical Studies*, no. 15). Bramcote, Notts, Grove Books 1978, pp. 32–51.

'This is the Word of the Lord', in G. J. Cuming, ed., *The Ministry of the Word. A Handbook to the 1978 Lectionary* (London, Bible Reading Fellowship and OUP 1979), pp. xvii–xx.

'ΔΙ' ΕΥΧΗΣ ΛΟΓΟΥ (Justin, Apology, i.66,2)', in *Journal of Theological Studies*, N.S. vol. xxxi, (1980), Pt 1 (April), pp. 80–2.

'Thmuis Revisited: Another Look at the Prayers of Bishop Sarapion', in *Theological Studies*, vol. 41 (1980), no. 3 (September), pp. 568–75.

(co-author with R. C. D. Jasper and others): *The Alternative Service Book 1980. A Commentary by the Liturgical Commission*, London, Church Information Office 1980.

(with S. G. Hall): art. 'Book of Common Prayer', in *Theologische Realenzyklopädie*, Bd. VII, Lieferung 11/2, ss. 80–3. Berlin and New York, Walter de Gruyter 1980.

'The Early Eucharistic Liturgies in Recent Research', in B. D. Spinks, ed., *'The Sacrifice of Praise: Essays in honour of Arthur Hubert Couratin* (Rome, Centro Liturgico Vincenziano 1981), pp. 63–9.

'ἐποτίσθημεν (1 Corinthians 12.13)', in *New Testament Studies*, 27/2 (Jan. 1981), pp. 283–5.

Letter (on the Prayer Book [Protection] Bill) in *Church Times*, No. 6167 (24 April 1981), p. 12.

''Η Καρποφορία. A Note', in *Ephemerides Liturgicae*, vol. xcv (1981), No. 6, pp. 556–8.

(Letter to the editor on) 'Theology and Sociology', in *Theology*, vol. lxxxv (1982) No. 704 (March), pp. 123–4.

A History of Anglican Liturgy (2nd edition), London, Macmillan 1982.

2   As Editor

The Durham Book; being the draft of the Revision of the Book of Common Prayer in 1661. London, OUP 1961 (also pub. London, The Alcuin Club, 1975).

Studies in Church History, vol. ii: *Papers read at the Second Winter and Summer Meetings of the Ecclesiastical History Society.* Leiden, E. J. Brill 1963.

Studies in Church History, vol. iii. Leiden, E. J. Brill, 1966.

The Province of York: Papers read at the Fifth Summer Meeting of the Ecclesiastical History Society (*Studies in Church History*), vol. iv. Leiden, E. J. Brill, 1967.

The Church and Academic Learning: Papers read at the Sixth Summer Meeting of the Ecclesiastical History Society (*Studies in Church History*), vol. v. Leiden, E. J. Brill 1969.

The Mission of the Church and the Propagation of the Faith: Papers read at the Seventh Summer Meeting and the Eighth Winter Meeting of the Ecclesiastical History Society (*Studies in Church History*), vol. vi. London, CUP 1970.

(with Derek Baker) *Councils and Assemblies: Papers read at the Eighth Summer and the Ninth Winter Meetings of the Ecclesiastical History Society* (*Studies in Church History*), vol. vii. London, CUP 1971.

(with Derek Baker) *Popular Beliefs and Practices: Papers read at the Ninth Summer Meeting and the Tenth Winter Meeting of the Ecclesiastical History Society* (*Studies in Church History*), vol. viii. London, CUP 1972.

(with R. C. D. Jasper) *Prayers of the Eucharist, Early and Reformed.* London, Collins, 1st ed. 1975, 2nd ed. 1980.

(also contributor) *Essays on Hippolytus* (*Grove Liturgical Study*, No. 15). Bramcote, Notts, Grove Books 1978.

(also contributor) *The Ministry of the Word. A Handbook to the 1978 Lectionary.* London, Bible Reading Fellowship and OUP 1979.

NOTES

1   The Spirit's Freedom in the Spirit's Framework

1   E.g. K. McDonnell (ed.), *The Holy Spirit and Power* (Doubleday & Co., New York 1975); J. Dorr, *Remove the Heart of Stone* (Gill & Macmillan Ltd., Dublin 1978); my *Pentecostal Anglicans* (Hodder 1982).

2   Rom. 8.15–16.

3   *The Sunday Service* (Methodist Publishing House 1975), p. B9.

4   Cardinal Suenens, *A New Pentecost?* (Darton, Longman & Todd 1975), p. 217.

5   ASB 1980, first and second eucharistic prayers, pp. 131 and 133.

6   One of the best books on this form of prayer is M. T. Kelsey, *Speaking with Tongues* (Epworth Press 1974).

7   'The Significance and Potential of Pentecostalism' by Peter Hocken in *New Heaven? New Earth?* by Simon Tugwell, Peter Hocken, George Every and John Orme Mills (Darton, Longman & Todd 1976), p. 31.

8   On this see B. Yocum, *Prophecy: Exercising the Prophetic Gifts of the Spirit in the Church Today* (Word of Life, Ann Arbor, Michigan 1976).

9   'Liturgy and Charisms' in K. McDonnell, op. cit., pp. 166–7.

10   M. Perham, *The Eucharist* (Alcuin Club Manual No. 1, SPCK 1978), p. 1.

11   P. Dearmer, *The Story of the Prayer Book* (OUP 1933), p. 11.

12   Patricia Beale and Martha Keys Barker, *The Folk Arts in Renewal* (Hodder & Stoughton 1980), p. 16.

13   *New Covenant*, vol. 5, no. 1 (July 1975), p. 24; *A New Canterbury Tale* (Grove Books 1978), pp. 29–33.

14   J. Gelineau, *The Liturgy Today and Tomorrow* (Darton, Longman & Todd 1978), p. 90.

15   *City of God*, 22. 8. On the *Jubilatio* see E. Ensley, *Sounds of Wonder* (Paulist Press, New York 1977).

16   E. B. Pusey, *Parochial Sermons* (revised ed., 1878), vol. 2, p. 254.

2   Initiation: Sacrament and Experience

1   For an example of Jesus being baptized as a boy, see the sarcophagus of S. Maria Antiqua, Rome, in J. G. Davies, *The Early*

Christian Church (London 1965), pl. 14. For the Baptist as the bishop, and the Jordan as the deacon, see the dome of the Baptistery of the Orthodox (wrongly restored) at Ravenna (ibid., pl. 5).

2 Cf. A. P. Milner, OP, *The Theology of Confirmation* (Cork 1972), pp. 83–95.

3 'Baptism and the Pagan Mysteries in the Fourth Century', in *The Heythrop Journal*, 13 (1972), pp. 247–67.

4 E: 'Baptism, Confirmation, and Holy Communion', in *The Alternative Service Book 1980* (London 1980). M: *The Methodist Service Book* (Methodist Publishing House 1975), in the rite entitled: 'The Baptism of those who are able to answer for themselves, with the Public Reception into Full Membership, or Confirmation'. C: *Rite of Christian Initiation of Adults*, Provisional Text, ICEL, Washington 1974.

3 *'Ye shall pray for ...':The Intercession*

1 Augustine, *2nd Letter to Proba*, VIII, 17, quoted by P. Baelz, *Prayer and Providence* (SCM 1968), p. 112, n. 22, where Baelz gives a paraphrase of the original; v. Migne, *Patrologia Latina*, 33, col. 501.

2 A. Bloom, *Living Prayer* (Libra Books 1966), p. 71.

3 G. Wainwright, *Doxology* (Epworth 1980), p. 355.

4 Quoted from M. Duggan, *Through the Year with Michael Ramsey* (Hodder and Stoughton 1975), p. 162.

5 M. Hatchett, *Commentary on the New American Prayer Book* (Seabury, 1980), pp. 374–5, 377–8.

6 U. Simon, 'Unliturgical Remarks on Eucharistic Liturgy', *Theology*, lxxiv, 611 (May 1971), p. 207.

7 P. De Clerck, *La 'prière universelle' dans les liturgies latines anciennes* (Aschendorff, Münster 1977), pp. 311f.

8 F. A. Iremonger, *William Temple* (OUP 1948), p. 327; Temple is quoted in some observations on the characteristics of Lancashire folk, but they can be applied less restrictedly!

9 *Rule of St Benedict*, ch. 20 ('Reverence in Prayer'); W. Perry, *The Scottish Prayer-Book – its Value and History* (CUP 1929), p. 54; Psalm 51.10.

10 P. A. H. De Boer, *Fatherhood and Motherhood in Israelite and Judaean Piety* (Brill, Leiden 1974), p. 53.

11 Kenneth Stevenson (ed.), *Authority and Freedom in the Liturgy* (Grove Liturgical Study 17, 1979), pp. 30f.

12 A. Michael Ramsey, *Jesus and the Living Past* (OUP 1980), p. 56, where Ramsey describes the more extreme variety of this tension as a 'spiritual *tour de force*'.

13 *The Book of Common Prayer* (Seabury 1979), pp. 383–95.

14 G. Willis, *Essays in Early Roman Liturgy* (Alcuin Club Collections 46) (London 1964), pp. 45–7.

15 H. Engberding, in various articles entitled 'Das anaphorische Fürbittgebet', in *Oriens Christianus*, e.g. on Armenian Basil, 51 (1967), pp. 29–50; others include 45 (1961), pp. 20–29; 46 (1962), pp. 33–60; 47 (1963), pp. 16–52; 49 (1965), pp. 18–37; and 50 (1966), pp. 13–18.

16 Wainwright, op. cit., pp. 42f; cf. F. Paget, *The Spirit of Discipline* (Longmans 1933), for the famous essay on *accidie*.

17 A. M. Allchin, *The World is a Wedding* (Darton, Longman and Todd 1978), pp. 68ff.

18 R. C. D. Jasper, G. J. Cuming (ed.), *The Prayers of the Eucharist* (Collins 1980²) pp. 36f; cf. J. Doresse, E. Lanne (ed.), *Un témoin archaïque de la liturgie copte de S. Basile* (Bibliothèque du Muséon 47, Louvain 1960), pp. 24ff.

19 The excellent little book, Michael Vasey, *Intercessions in Worship*, Grove Worship Booklet 77 (Grove Books 1981), is a notable exception; a more general work is Lukas Vischer, *Intercession* (WCC 1980), combining profundity with constructive and eirenic comment.

4 *The Eucharistic Prayer: Tradition and Development*

1 L. L. Mitchell, 'The Alexandrine Anaphora of St Basil of Caesarea: Ancient Source of "A Common Eucharistic Prayer",' *Anglican Theological Review*, lviii. 2 (April 1976), p. 195.

2 Joseph Heinemann, *Prayer in the Talmud. Studia Judaica*, Band IX. Berlin/New York 1977.

3 This point of view has been associated recently with J.-P. Audet, 'Literary Forms and Contents of a Normal *Eucharistia* in the First Century', *Studia Evangelica. Texte u. Untersuchungen* 73 (Berlin 1959), pp. 643–62. Heinemann brings some further precisions to my own consideration of this matter, 'The Eucharistic Prayer of the Ancient Church According to Recent Research: Results and Reflections', *Studia Liturgica* 11 (1976), pp. 138–58. (A slightly expanded text of this paper appeared as 'From *Berakah* to *Eucharistia*: A Reopening Question', *Worship* 50 (1976), pp. 115–37.)

4 For the text, see R. H. Charles, *The Book of Jubilees or The Little Genesis* (London 1902), p. 138. (Chap. xxii, vv. 5–9).

5 Heinemann, op. cit., p. 33.

6 Henri Cazelles, 'L'Anaphore et l'Ancien Testament', *Eucharisties d'Orient et d'Occident. Lex Orandi* 46 (Paris 1970), pp. 11–21; also 'Eucharistie, bénédiction et sacrifice dans l'Ancien Testament', *La Maison-Dieu* 123 (1975), pp. 7–28. Jean Laporte, *La doctrine eucharistique chez Philon d'Alexandre*. Paris 1972.

7 *Spec. leg.* 2.146–9.

8   L. Ligier, 'The Origins of the Eucharistic Prayer: From the Last Supper to the Eucharist', *Studia Liturgica* 9 (1973), pp. 176–85.

9   E. Kilmartin, 'Sacrificium Laudis: Content and Function of Early Eucharistic Prayers', *Theological Studies* 35 (1974), p. 280.

10 G. J. Cuming, 'The Anaphora of St Mark, A Study in Development'. A Paper delivered in the Liturgy Master Theme at the Eighth International Conference on Patristic Studies at Oxford in 1979, forthcoming in *Le Muséon*; see also W. H. Bates, 'Thanksgiving and Intercession in the Liturgy of St Mark', in Bryan D. Spinks (ed.), *The Sacrifice of Praise*, CLV, Rome 1981, pp. 107–19; H. A. J. Wegman, 'Une Anaphore Incomplete?', in R. Van Den Broek and M. J. Vermaseren (eds.), *Studies in Gnosticism and Religions*, Leiden 1981, pp. 432–50.

11 Wm Macomber, 'The Maronite and Chaldean Versions of the Anaphora of the Apostles', *Orientalia Christiana Periodica* 37 (1971), pp. 58–66. This point was urged somewhat more strongly by Dr Macomber at the Dumbarton Oaks Symposium in May 1980, where he presented a (presently unpublished) reconstruction of the original text of the Anaphora of the Apostles.

12 Bryan D. Spinks, 'The Original Form of the Anaphora of the Apostles: A Suggestion in the Light of Maronite Sharar', *Ephemerides Liturgicae* 91 (1977), pp. 146–61.

13 Op. cit. (note 11 above).

14 Bryan D. Spinks, 'The Jewish Sources for the Sanctus', *The Heythrop Journal* 21 (1980), p. 173.

15 Hans-Jörg Auf der Maur, *Die Osterhomilien des Asterios Sophistes als Quelle für die Geschichte der Osterfeier. Trierer theologische Studien*, Band 19 (Trier 1967), pp. 74–94.

16 Cuming, op. cit. (note 10 above).

17 Aidan Kavanagh, OSB, 'Thoughts on the New Eucharistic Prayers', *Worship* 43 (1969), pp. 2–12; Richard Albertine, MM, 'Problem of the (Double) Epiclesis in the New Roman Eucharistic Prayers', *Ephemerides Liturgicae* 91 (1977), pp. 193–202; Hans-Joachim Schulz, *Ökumenische Glaubenseinheit aus eucharistischer Überlieferung. Konfessionskundliche u. kontroverstheologische Studien*, Band 39 (Paderborn 1976), pp. 56–72.

18 *DACL* I.1892. L. Duchesne, *Christian Worship, Its Origin and Evolution*. Fifth edition (London 1949), pp. 181f.

19 For a particularly valuable study of this matter, see the work of Hans-Joachim Schulz cited in note 17 above. This received serious criticism from the theological perspective by B. Schultze, *Orientalia Christiana Periodica* 44 (1978), pp. 273–308, to which Schulz responded in, 'Liturgischer Vollzug und sakramentale Wirklichkeit des eucharistischen Opfers', *Orientalia Christiana Periodica* 45 (1979), pp. 245–66. I am indebted to Prof. Robert Taft for drawing my

attention to this discussion. Cf. also Kenneth Stevenson, '"Anaphoral Offering": some observations on Eastern Eucharistic Prayers,' in *Ephemerides Liturgicae*, 94 (1980), pp. 209–28.

20   A. Kavanagh, op. cit. (note 17 above).

21   On this prayer, see the article of L. L. Mitchell cited in note 1 above. The full article occupies pp. 194–206.

5   Shape and Liturgy

1   E. M. Forster, *Aspects of the Novel*, Pelican edn 1968, p. 45. On another way of constructing a sequence, not strictly narrative, cf. G. J. Cuming, 'The Text of "Messiah"', *Music and Letters* 31 (1950), pp. 226–30.

2   See E. C. Ratcliff, 'The Communion Service of the Prayer Book' in *Chichester Diocesan Gazette*, 16 (1935), pp. 7–12, 102–8 (reprinted in his *Reflections on Liturgical Revision*, Grove Liturgical Study 22, Bramcote Notts 1980, pp. 12–19).

3   R. H. Connolly and H. W. Codrington, ed., *Two Commentaries on the Jacobite Liturgy*, London Text and Translation Soc. 1913; George, pp. 11–23, Moses, pp. 24–90. On Dionysius, see D. Rutledge, *Cosmic Theology*, London 1964.

4   N. Cabasilas, *Commentary on the Divine Liturgy*, J. M. Hussey and P. A. McNulty, tr., London 1960; N. V. Gogol, *The Divine Liturgy*, R. Edmonds, tr., London 1960.

5   See J. Schérer, ed., *Entretien d'Origène avec Héraclide*, Paris 1960, pp. 62–5. Text reconstructed by P. Nautin in his *Lettres et écrivains chrétiens du 2ᵉ siècle*, ch. 12.

6   (a) Calvin, Knox; (b) British Methodist 1975; (c) John Chrysostom, etc.; (d) Roman Canon, English Anglican 1980; (e) British Methodist 1936, 2nd order. Other possibilities, see G. J. Cuming and R. C. D. Jasper, *Prayers of the Eucharist, Early and Reformed*, London 1975, 1980; other dimensions, cf. R. F. Buxton, *Eucharist and Institution Narrative*, Alcuin Club Collections 58, Great Wakering 1976.

7   A. Vööbus, 'Kritische Beobachtungen über die lukanische Darstellung des Abendmahls', *Zeitschrift für die neutestamentliche Wissenschaft*, 61 (1970), pp. 102–10.

8   *Service for the First Two Nights of Passover*, J. Schlesinger, Vienna 1930, p. 33.

9   Notably the Rev. Ronald Freeman, of Tottington (Lancs).

10   R. Otto, *Zur Erneuerung und Ansgestaltung des Gottesdienstes* (= *Aus der Welt der Religion*, liturgische Reihe, Heft 2, Giessen 1925), pp. 45–7. His argument (p. 47) that the second cup had no reference to the Passion is less compelling.

11   Cf. J. Quasten, *Musik und Gesang in den Kulten der heidnischen Antike und christlichen Frühzeit*, Münster/Westf. 1930. Note Morton Smith,

'Pauline Worship as Seen by Pagans', *Harvard Theological Review* 73 (1980) 1–2 (Jan.–Apr.), pp. 241–9.

12 Cf. G. J. Cuming, 'Service-endings in the Epistles', *New Testament Studies* 22 (1975), pp. 110–13.

13 Cf. G. J. Cuming, 'ἐποτίσθημεν (1 Corinthians 12.13)', *New Testament Studies* 27:2 (Jan. 1981), pp. 283–5.

6 The Shape of the Eucharist: A Survey and Appraisal

1 Because a solemn 'well behaved' religious meal simply would not translate from a Jewish into a pagan context? I Corinthians 11.17–22 seems evidence for this.

2 This seems to mirror the way in which in the New Testament the Church occupies the same place that the human family did in Judaism, a change in which the eschatological climate early Christians saw themselves living in no doubt contributed. Jesus' own attitude to the ordinary human family seems to have been distinctly ambivalent at times; see for example Mark 3. 31–5.

3 Justin Martyr, *First Apology*, 67, 1–3, quoted from R. C. D. Jasper and G. J. Cuming, *Prayers of the Eucharist*, 1st ed., Collins 1975 pp. 19–20.

4 The fact that modern-liturgy makers have used Justin as one of their models heightens the similarity.

5 For a conveniently accessible text of some of this fascinating document see Jasper and Cuming, op. cit., pp. 111–15; the full Latin text can be found in M. Andrieu, *Les Ordines Romani du Haut Moyen Age*, vol. II; a Latin text with English translation in E. G. C. F. Atchley, *Ordo Romanus Primus*, De La More 1905.

6 Witness the former Bishop of Chester's apparent insistence that liturgical vesture should be worn by the president on such occasions.

7 See G. Dix, *The Shape of the Liturgy*, Dacre Press 1945, pp. 522–6.

8 A priest who celebrates the ministry of the word from his stall in the choir or from the chancel step, and then, for the ministry of the sacrament, disappears up a long Gothic chancel in order to slide behind an altar pulled just sufficiently far away from the east wall of the church to enable him to do this has no appreciation of the real significance of the change from eastward to westward facing, and does not know what he is doing.

9 This is argued in detail by J. I. Packer in his introduction to *The Work of Thomas Cranmer*, Courtenay Library of Reformation Classics, p. xxvi.

10 When the history of the twentieth-century Church of England comes to be written, it will be one of Colin Buchanan's enduring claims to fame that he made its Evangelicals take liturgy seriously (I mean as worship, not as a quarry for Protestant polemic or as

proofs of impeccable doctrinal rectitude). One only hopes that students at St John's College, Nottingham, who have the great privilege of being taught liturgy by him, appreciate what it is that they are getting.

11 That it is a revolution is demonstrated by Lefèbvrist works such as Michael Davies' *Pope Paul's New Mass*. If you start from the position that the Tridentine-medieval position is the faith once delivered to the saints you are bound to see the post-Vatican II liturgical reforms as a repudiation of it (perhaps only a partial one?). If you do not start from this premise, you reach quite a different conclusion! One suspects there must still be a great deal of historical and doctrinal reappraisal to come around these issues in the Roman Catholic Church. No church finds it easy to admit that it has ever made serious doctrinal mistakes, but those that claim to be infallible inevitably find it more difficult than most.

12 Only the Church of England could invent such a singularly inelegant name for a liturgical book! Why could it not have been called 'The Book of Common Prayer, 1980' and given the subtitle 'An Alternative to 1662'? No one yet seems to have pointed out another strange result of the process of liturgical revision that has led to the ASB. Until about the middle of the 1960s the impetus for liturgical revision of the Eucharist in the Church of England was dissatisfaction, implicit or explicit, with the doctrine of the Prayer Book rite. At that time the emphasis changed to the language of the rite, without anyone appearing to notice that this was happening, and as far as the Eucharist is concerned the political composition and processes of the Church of England have ensured that it now has a rite in modern language that operates within the same doctrinal parameters as 1662, albeit possessing classical shape. Thus the end product of many years' pressure for doctrinal change is a rite of unchanged doctrine, but a new language and shape!

13 Cf. Kenneth Stevenson, *Gregory Dix – 25 Years On*, Grove Liturgical Study 10, Bramcote, Notts 1977.

14 The work of the former has not always been able to prevail in the decisions reached by the latter, alas!

7 Between God and World

1 For more detailed treatment of some of these questions, see my *Doxology* (London, Epworth, and New York, OUP 1980), especially Chapters 11 and 12. Note the still classic work of A. G. Hebert, *Liturgy and Society* (London, Faber 1935). Further: K. Barth, *Church Dogmatics* IV/2 (original 1955; ET Edinburgh, T. & T. Clark 1958), pp. 695–824 (ET pp. 614–726: 'The Holy Spirit and the upbuilding of the Christian community'); B. Wicker, *Culture and Liturgy* (London, Sheed and Ward 1963); J. J. von Allmen, *Worship: its theology and practice* (London, Lutterworth 1965), especially Chapters 1–5; A.

Schmemann, *The World as Sacrament* (London, Darton, Longman & Todd 1966); J. G. Davies, *Worship and Mission* (London, SCM 1966).

2 N. A. Nissiotis, 'Worship, eucharist and "intercommunion": an Orthodox reflection' in *Studia Liturgica* 2 (1963), pp. 193–222, in particular p. 201.

3 E. Jüngel, 'Die Autorität des bittenden Christus' in *Unterwegs zur Sache* (Munich, Kaiser 1972), pp. 187f.

4 G. Gutiérrez, *A Theology of Liberation* (ET, London, SCM 1973), p. 137, cf. pp. 262–5.

5 C. K. Barrett, *A Commentary on the Epistle to the Romans* (London, Black 1957), pp. 23f.

6 L. Newbigin, *The Open Secret: Sketches for a Missionary Theology* (London, SPCK 1978).

7 For nuances, see my *Eucharist and Eschatology* (London, Epworth 1978[3]), pp. 128–35.

8 J. H. Hick, *God and the Universe of Faiths* (London, Macmillan 1973).

9 H. Richard Niebuhr, *Christ and Culture* (New York, Harper and Row 1951). Serious reflection on our question is found in the Grove booklet by P. R. Akehurst and R. W. F. Wootton, *Inter-faith Worship?* (Bramcote, Grove 1977). Cf. Bryan Spinks, 'The Anaphora for India: Some Theological Objections to an attempt at Inculturation', in *Ephemerides Liturgicae*, 95,6 (1981), pp. 529–49.

10 E. Jüngel, 'Erwägungen zur Grundlegung evangelischer Ethik' in *Unterwegs zur Sache* (see note 3), especially pp. 244f. Jüngel says that 'to be condemned to pass away is thus in truth to be set free to become'. It is from the Yes which God said to the world in Christ that the light of promise falls on every honourable yes which the world says to itself in love, peace, compassion, freedom and justice.

11 For a full study, see G. P. Wiles, *Paul's Intercessory Prayers* (Cambridge, CUP 1974). Wiles summarizes thus: 'Signs are present throughout the letters that Paul believed himself appointed a mediator between God and the churches in his care, charged with the priestly responsibility of presenting them blameless to God at the parousia. The indications are sufficiently clear and frequent to reveal a deep intercessory sense lying behind all his preaching, teaching, prophesying, and pastoral work, adding new dimensions of meaning and urgency. While such mediation was clearly only one aspect of his complex apostolate, yet it seemed to lie near the heart of his self-understanding, a basic consequence of the intercessory act of God in Christ, an extension of the intercessory ministry of the exalted Christ (Romans 8.34) and of the indwelling Spirit (Romans 8.15f, 23, 26f; Galatians 4.6).'

12 K. P. Nickle, *The Collection* (London, SCM 1966).

13 See (and use) *For all God's people* (London, SPCK 1978). The

theological background is supplied in L. Vischer, *Intercession* (1980 = Faith and Order Paper No. 95).

14 Plenty of examples can be found in P. de Clerck, *La 'prière universelle' dans les liturgies latines anciennes* (Münster, Aschendorff 1977).

15 In Chapter 32 of his *Apology*, Tertullian says that it is Christian prayer for the emperor which holds back the final catastrophe. It became a commonplace to equate the continuance of the Roman empire – identified with the last of the kingdoms in Daniel 2.36ff – with the continuance of the world. In *Christ and Time* (ET London, SCM 1951), pp. 164–6, O. Cullmann cites Theodore of Mopsuestia, Theodoret and Calvin for the view that the 'restraining agents' in 2 Thessalonians 2.6f are the Christian missionary preaching and preacher (cf. Matthew 24.14: 'And this gospel of the kingdom will be preached throughout the whole world, as a testimony to all nations; and then the end will come').

16 On this passage, see E. Käsemann, *Perspectives on Paul* (ET London, SCM 1971), pp. 122–37. Käsemann suggests that Paul was critically reinterpreting glossolalic prayer by letting it be, like the other groanings, a mark of the 'not yet'.

17 E. Käsemann, for instance, shows great ethical sensitivity in his essay on 'divine service in the everyday world' yet cannot abide what he pejoratively calls 'the cult': see his exegesis of Romans 12.1f in *New Testament Questions of Today* (ET London, SCM 1969), pp. 188–95.

8 Worship and Theology

1 Cf. E. C. Ratcliff, *Liturgical Studies*, ed. A. H. Couratin and D. H. Tripp (SPCK 1976), pp. 213–16.

2 Quoted with many other examples in J. A. Jungmann, *The Mass of the Roman Rite*, ad loc.

9 Reform of Symbols in Roman Catholic Worship: Loss or Gain?

1 Cf. J. A. Jungmann, *The Mass of the Roman Rite*, vol. ii (ET New York, Benziger 1955), p. 271, n. 61.

2 Usage attested as early as 7th cent. in Roman stational liturgy; cf. Jungmann, op. cit., vol. ii (New York, Benziger 1951), p. 68.

3 Cf. my paper 'Baptismal exorcism in the Catholic Baptismal Rites after Vatican II', in *Studia Liturgica* 10 (1974), pp. 48–55.

4 B. Kleinheyer, *Die Priesterweihe in römischen Ritus. Eine liturgiehistorische Studie* = *Trierer Theologische Studien* 12 (Trier 1962). On secondary use of imposition of hands, cf. pp. 208–11. The subsequent criticism, that as a result of this lightening there is now in the rite for the ordering of priests no place for affirming the power to remit sins, except in the suggested form of homily, seems

to be justified.

5 This thesis, which is not undisputed, goes back to J. B. de Rossi; cf. L. Bouwens, art. 'Alfabet' in *Liturgisch Woordenboek* (Roermond 1958–68), p. 87f. See also now Z. Obertynski, ed., *The Cracow Pontifical* (= Henry Bradshaw Society, vol. 100, 1977); the form of alphabet there (p. 38 and *Tafel* IV, *Bild* V) may betray Etruscan influence; in view of the well-known role of the Etruscan learning in Roman society, survival of Etruscan writing is most probable in the context of conveyancing, surveying, etc. (Tr.)

6 Post-conciliar documents, in various ways, while favouring *celebratio versus populum*, carefully avoid giving it a monopoly.

7 For the historical background on the question of the celebrant facing towards or away from the people, cf O. Nussbaum, *Der Standort des Liturgen am christlichen Altar vor dem Jahr 1000. Eine archäologische und liturgiegeschichtliche Untersuchung = Theophaneia* 18.1/2, Bonn 1965.

8 Cf. Th. v. Boggay, art. 'Hetoimasia' in *Reallexikon zur byzantinischen Kunst* 2 (1971), pp. 1189–1202.

9 *Missale Romanum* 1970, Inst. Gen. 240 says in as many words: '*Formam ratione signi pleniorem habet Communio cum fit sub utraque specie*'.

10 The important assertion that the Mass had forfeited important features '*temporum iniuria*' was made by the Council itself in art. 50 of the Liturgy Constitution.

11 Pius XII, Encyclical letter, *Mediator Dei*; in A. Bugnini, ed., *Documenta Pontificia ad instaurationem liturgicam spectantia* (Rome 1953), p. 136ff. In this connection, note a dictum on liturgical sensitivity, of amazing penetration for the time (1947) and for the author: '*Non facile spernere, quidquid sacra liturgia suadeat*' (120; p. 138).

12 Liturgy Constitution. art. 55.

13 While the Liturgy Constitution (art. 57) describes concelebration rather dismissively as a sign of *unitas sacerdotii*, Cardinal Giacomo Lercaro, in a letter which he wrote as chairman of the Consilium for the Execution of the Liturgy Constitution to the presidents of the Bishops' Conferences on 30 June 1965 speaks of it as: '*manifestation de l'unité du sacrifice et du sacerdoce, de l'unité de tout le peuple de Dieu dans l'action sacrée*'.

14 *Missale Romanum* 1970, *Ordo Missae* n. 6: *tunc sacerdos, manibus extensis, dicit orationem* (p. 387).

15 The Assyrian word for 'pray' is equivalent to 'open the hands'. See S. Langdon, 'Gesture in Sumerian and Babylonian prayer', in *Journal of the Royal Asiatic Society* 1919, p. 541.

16 *Ordo Baptismi Parvulorum*, Rome ²1973, p. 18.

17 Cf. F. J. Dölger, 'Die Segnung der Kinder mit dem Kreuzzeichen in

der häuslichen Frömmigkeitsübung der Familie' in *Jahrbuch für Antike und Christentum* 8/9 (1965/6), pp. 42–5.

18 *Ordo Poenitentiae*, Rome 1974, n. 46.

19 In the *editio typica* of the *Rituale Romanum* of 1925 the prayer before the anointings was (a restoration at so early a date) at least to be said *'extensa manu dextera super caput infirmi'* (n. 7).

20 Cf. *Ordo Unctionis Infirmorum*, Rome 1972, n. 74.

10 The Liturgical Use and Abuse of Patristics

1 Some of these developments are conveniently documented in J. G. Davies, 'The Introduction of the Numinous into the Liturgy: an Historical Note', *Studia Liturgica* 8 (1971/2), pp. 216–23.

2 Tertullian, *De Anima* 9.

3 E. C. Ratcliff, 'The Sanctus and the Pattern of the Early Anaphora', *Journal of Ecclesiastical History* 1 (1950), reprinted in *Liturgical Studies*, ed. A. H. Couratin and D. H. Tripp (London, SPCK 1976), p. 19.

4 Ibid., pp. 26–7.

5 A. H. Couratin, 'The Sacrifice of Praise', *Theology* 58 (1955), pp. 285–91; G. A. Michell, *Landmarks in Liturgy* (London, Darton, Longman & Todd 1961), pp. 84–9.

6 See for example J. G. Davies, 'Criticisms of "An Experimental Liturgy"', *Theology* 62 (1959), pp. 276–7.

7 See C. O. Buchanan, 'Series 3 in the Setting of the Anglican Communion', in *The Eucharist Today*, ed. R. C. D. Jasper (London, SPCK 1974), pp. 15–16, and esp. nn. 39, 40.

8 A. F. Walls, 'The Latin version of Hippolytus' *Apostolic Tradition'*, in *Studia Patristica* 3 (1961), pp. 155–62; E. Segelberg, 'The Ordination Prayers in Hippolytus', in *Studia Patristica* 13 (1975), pp. 397–408; P. F. Bradshaw, 'Ordination', in *Essays on Hippolytus* ed. Geoffrey J. Cuming (Bramcote, Grove 1978), pp. 33–8.

9 Gregory Dix, *The Shape of the Liturgy* (London, Dacre/Black 1945), p. 264.

10 J. A. Jungmann, *The Early Liturgy to the Time of Gregory the Great* (London, Darton, Longman & Todd 1960), p. 8.

11 See C. O. Buchanan, *Modern Anglican Liturgies 1958–1968* (London, OUP 1968), pp. 118–21.

12 *An Order for Holy Communion*, A Report of the Church of England Liturgical Commission (1966), p. viii.

13 Conveniently outlined by J. L. Houlden, 'Sacrifice and the Eucharist', in *Thinking about the Eucharist*, papers by members of the Church of England Doctrine Commission (London, SCM 1972), pp. 81–98.

14 Anglican–Roman Catholic International Commission, *Statement on the Eucharist* (1971), section 5.

15 J. L. Houlden, 'Liturgy and her Companions', in *The Eucharist Today*, pp. 168–76; T. G. A. Baker, *Questioning Worship* (London, SCM 1977).

16 On this see my essay, 'Authority and Freedom in the Early Liturgy', in *Authority and Freedom in Liturgy*, ed. Kenneth Stevenson (Bramcote, Grove 1979), pp. 4–10.

17 Cf. Kenneth Stevenson, 'Stretching Worship', *Theology 84*, 690 (1981), pp. 11–16.

11 Liturgical Revision in the Church of England in Retrospect

1 The 'epitaph' was of course commissioned before the end had finally come, but as the outcome was predictable, and few would have wanted the then-current course of liturgical revision to go indefinitely into the future, the commissioning of an epitaph whilst the subject of it was still alive did not have the same distressing character that it would have with human beings.

2 The text of this was published in B. J. Wigan (ed.), *The Liturgy in English* (OUP 1962), and it went through three editions between 1950 and 1963. Its history has been recorded in T. S. Garrett, *Worship in the Church of South India* (Lutterworth 1958) and L. W. Brown, *Relevant Liturgy* (SPCK 1965).

3 Cf. Garrett, op. cit., pp. 13–14. The actual use of Dix's 'Shape' (modified) I traced out in *Modern Anglican Liturgies 1958–1968* (OUP 1968) and in 'Series 3 in the Setting of the Anglican Communion' in R. C. D. Jasper (ed.), *The Eucharist Today: Studies on Series 3* (SPCK 1974), p. 13.

4 Obvious instances were Canada (1959), West Indies (1959), Japan (1959), and the Church of India, Pakistan, Burma, and Ceylon (1960). The texts of each of these is in Wigan, op. cit.

5 His own account is to be found in Brown, op. cit. Mine is in *Modern Anglican Liturgies 1958–1968*, chs. 2 and 3, and in *The Eucharist Today*, pp. 13–14.

6 Ratcliff's articles in the *Journal of Ecclesiastical History* in 1950 are reprinted in A. H. Couratin and D. H. Tripp (eds), *E. C. Ratcliff: Liturgical Studies* (SPCK 1976) with others which show the desiderata he cherished. A further view of his principles is afforded in D. H. Tripp (ed.), *E. C. Ratcliff: Reflections on Liturgical Revision* (Grove Liturgical Study no. 22, Grove Books 1980). Couratin's views are to be found in his articles in *Theology* in 1955, his essay in D. M. Paton (ed.), *The Parish Communion Today* (SPCK 1962) and, up to a point, in the Liturgical Commission's production *Reshaping the Liturgy* (CIO 1964). But most of his writings on any liturgical subject (as, for instance, his contribution to the Pelican series on Historical Theology) betray his mind fairly clearly. We now also have further insights into his thinking in Bryan Spinks (ed.), *The Sacrifice of Praise* (CLV, Rome 1981), a collection of essays in honour of Arthur Couratin.

7   That is to say that the Prayer Book (Alternative and Other Services) Measure 1965 gained the Royal Assent in March 1965 and came into force in May 1966, and gave a period of revision which would have expired in 1980 if it had not been overtaken by the more thoroughgoing Church of England (Worship and Doctrine) Measure 1974, which came into force on 1 September 1975. (The text of this is in my *Supplement for 1973–4 to Recent Liturgical Revision in the Church of England* (Grove Booklet on Ministry and Worship no. 14a, Grove Books 1974).

8   The first stages of vernacular usage in England by *Roman Catholics* involved 'Thou' form texts (roughly covering the second half of the 1960s), and the later stages, from the coming of ICEL in 1968 and the new Mass in 1970, have been generally using 'You' form texts (though rarely in the Lord's Prayer).
The first *Anglicans* to address God as 'You' were Australians and New Zealanders, both in 1966 (see *Modern Anglican Liturgies 1958–1968*, p. 4). But my second collection, *Further Anglican Liturgies 1968–1975* (Grove Books 1975), shows a virtually unbroken 'You' usage in all the modern texts it presents. Thus 1968 is the hinge year.
The *Methodist Sunday Service* authorized in 1968 had 'Thou' and 'you' in parallel columns – a diglot version! It had to, *because it came in 1968*. The later Methodist revisions have been wholly 'You' form.

9   As to text, the American rites have removed 'men' from the creed ('Who for us *men* and for our salvation . . .'). As to rubrics, Rite A declines to say '*he*' in the rubrics, unless the 'president' is thereby meant. And, at the time of writing, all English Anglican presidents of the Eucharist are male. No one in England has started yet on the American venture of deleting all suggestion that God is male – 'Our parent in heaven . . .').

10 Series 2 communion was thought highly permissive when it first came out, but with hindsight it now appears a highly disciplined rite. The coming of the Series 3 range of services was marked by a blessed innovation for the Church of England – opening 'Notes'. These left the text relatively clean, but gave permission for many variant uses. When Rite A has come along, not only are there two different positions for penitence, and four eucharistic prayers in the main text (with a fifth, of a sort, in the BCP pattern, and a sixth in an appendix), but also there is constant provision for the various ministers to use their own words, or '*other suitable forms*'.

11 Series 2 provided for an optional versicle and response, often said with the congregation still kneeling after the confession and absolution. Series 3 made the Peace mandatory, strongly suggested standing for it, and by 'Note' permitted the passing of a greeting and action through the congregation. Rite A provides two

alternative sets of presidential words in the main text, with a supply of seasonal variants in an appendix, and makes suggestions about 'passing' (or, rather, as it now is, 'exchanging') the Peace in the main text. It also provides by 'Note' for it to be used in other places in the rite when so desired. See my *The Kiss of Peace* (Grove Books 1982).

12   The obvious such situations are the provision of a Thanksgiving after the Birth of a Child and the Renewal of Baptismal Vows. At the very end of the 1970s – after the ASB had been completed – the Commission also went to work on the provision of more imaginative liturgical uses for the benefit of the sick. At the time of writing this report had just been published, but not been debated in Synod.

13   This happened on 10 November 1971. Fortunately the Synod ran out of time halfway through the eucharistic prayer, and thus David Frost's first post-communion prayer (for instance) was saved for a later day when Synod had recovered slightly from its bout of instant amending. (David Frost's own account is worth reading – see his *The Language of Series 3* (Grove Booklet on Ministry and Worship no. 12, Grove Books, 1973).)

14   In theory this power is limited – the members can only make proposals in respect of those parts of the text concerning which amendments had been sent to the Revision Committee, so that no new questions could be opened. As will appear a few lines further on, by the end of the 1970s virtually every line of a service prepared by the Commission became the subject of amendments and suggestions to the Revision Committee, so that there was in turn no restriction upon the back-bench amendments in full Synod at the revision stage.

15   The House of Bishops was tempted into ill-advised action by the late Bishop of Leicester, Dr Ronald Williams, in 1976, when it restored two lines to the Prayer of Humble Access in '1½', as a bracketed option (by a majority of *one* in the House of Bishops), – see ASB, p. 188. They also acted stupidly in relation to the word 'Offertory' in the same rite (ASB, p. 189). Consequently they almost lost the rite at Final Approval – Synod being very irritated indeed. Impenitently they then did the same with the Calendar and Lectionary in 1978, and, after General Synod had rejected Josephine Butler from the second division of the saintly league-table by 120 votes to 117, restored the good lady (see ASB, p. 21) – again by a majority of *one*! Synod then turned and berated the pink-faced bishops roundly, and has now changed this feature of Standing Orders.

16   This Measure (the full title of which is The Church of England (Worship and Doctrine) Measure 1974) superseded the Alternative Services Measure from 1 September 1975. Its text is printed in my *Supplement for 1973–4 to Recent Liturgical Revision in the Church of*

England (Grove Booklet on Ministry and Worship no. 14a, Grove Books, 1974).

17 It was at this session of General Synod that the major decision to work for a 'People's Service Book' in 1980 was taken.

18 The actual number of days for each Revision Committee is shown on the chart. To this must be added vast correspondence, travelling time for the far-flung (there was no Diocese of Europe in those days . . .), and hard work in redrafting between meetings for the Steering Committee handful within the Revision Committee, and for the much-pressurized and little-recognized secretariat.

19 This was published in time for the Lambeth Conference of 1968, and included texts which the Church of England Commission was submitting to the initial meetings of 'ICET' (the International Consultation on English Texts). The texts were for discussion and study only – no steps were being taken at that stage to authorize them for use.

20 His original second line read 'Jesus, bearer of the world's sin . . .' and ICET altered it to 'bearer of our sins'.

21 This was a happy stretching of a point. Resident in Oxford, he journeyed to King's College each week to teach, and thus qualified for the University seat. Ronald Jasper had vacated the seat in 1970.

22 The occasions which come to mind are the tidying of the untidy – whether of 'adaptations' or the 'rag-bag'. This last was a series of miscellaneous proposals designed to pull together the contents of the ASB at the last stages, and to rescue some bits which were in danger of getting lost.

23 *The Proposed Book of Common Prayer* of the American Episcopal Church was authorized at the General Convention in 1976, and published in 1977. The word *'proposed'* was deleted from the title at the next General Convention in 1979. It is now *'the'* Book.

24 *An Australian Prayer Book* was authorized by General Synod in 1977 and published in 1978. It is alternative to the BCP.

25 In the twelve months from November 1979 to November 1980 there flowed from the anti-ASB lobby: a special journal number (*PN Review 13*) containing vast 'Petitions' to General Synod; a series of articles in *The Daily Telegraph* (and elsewhere); a 'gallup poll'; a symposium (*Ritual Murder*, ed. Brian Morris (Carcanet Press, Manchester 1980)); and an inquiry into the churches of one archdeaconry, to mention but the most notable of their products.

26 Apart from the Commission's *Commentary*, the unofficial *Anglican Worship Today* was published on 10 November 1980, and commentaries on separate services both already exist and are likely to increase considerably.

27 *Episcopal Services* (published in December 1980) is a joint production of the Alcuin Club and the Church Literature Association. Its blurb

on the outside back-cover indicates that its purpose is to save bishops having to 'work out a whole series of ceremonial details for themselves'. One can only fervently hope that the advice contained in this extraordinary publication will redouble every bishop's determination to work out for himself what he is going to do in church.

28 This was the sort of task the *Growing into Union* team attempted, and since our dispersion (which was only geographical, but nevertheless fatal to our continuance) there has been little similar endeavour.

29 See also note 12 above.

INDEX

179